EXPLORING CAREERS IN
CHILD CARE

EXPLORING CAREERS IN
CHILD CARE
CINCINNATI PUBLIC SCHOOLS

HOME ECONOMICS DEPARTMENT
230 EAST 9th STREET
CINCINNATI, OHIO 45202

MARILYN KAY McFARLAND, Instructional Consultant
MARIALYCE KNOLL, Field Test Coordinator.

226536

A McKNIGHT HOME ECONOMICS CAREER PROGRAM
McKNIGHT PUBLISHING COMPANY, BLOOMINGTON ILLINOIS

FIFTH EDITION

Lithographed in U.S.A.

PUBLISHING COMPANY/BLOOMINGTON, ILLINOIS 61701

Ronald E. Dale, Vice President - Editorial, wishes to acknowledge the skills and talents of the following people and organizations in the preparation of this publication.

Carol Bixler
Home Economist/Writer

Michael Crowe
Staff Writer

Cheri Brueggemann
Developmental Network Coordinator

Phyllis Norfleet
Secretarial Assistant

Karen Ament
Mary Catherine Fairfield
Nadine Fred
Laura Harper
Researchers

Carolyn Beehn
Genny Davis
Typists

Gorman's Typesetting
M. R. Typography
Composition

R. R. Donnelley & Sons
Preproduction and Printing

Donna M. Faull
Production Editor

Bettye King
Copy Editor

Elizabeth Purcell
Art Editor/Layout Artist

R. Scott Jones
Staff Illustrator

Linda Hoerner
Jeannie Lanham
Production Coordinators

Sue Whitsett
Proofreader

Ron Steege
Graphic Designer

Curt Beamer
Photographer

William McKnight III
Manufacturing

Library of Congress
Card Catalog Number: 74-82448

SBN: 87345-573-8

First and Second Editions 1970: Cincinnati Public Schools under a grant from the Ohio Department of Education, Division of Vocational Education

Third Edition 1972: McKnight Publishing Company/Cincinnati Public Schools and Field Test Teachers — Local Field Test

Fourth Edition 1973: McKnight Publishing Company/Cincinnati Public Schools — National Field Test

Fifth Edition 1974: Revision based on feedback from National Field Test to meet the needs of students

Foreword

The **Exploring Careers in Child Care** program is the first of a series of career development programs to be published. These programs are the result of a dream by the Cincinnati Home Economics Department to develop a home economics curriculum that would prepare junior high students better for the 1980's.

The Cincinnati Public Schools became aware in 1969 that the home economics curriculum would not meet this goal. The approach had to change. This recognized need for change was based on several observations. One factor, obviously, was the recognition of the rapid changes taking place in the family living pattern. In addition, the teachers' analyses of student behavior problems revealed that many of the pupils felt that home economics was very critical of their personal living patterns, while other groups saw no functional value in many of the home economics activities. Students retaliated: some with indifference; others with nonparticipation or antagonism. Furthermore, students, parents, and teachers were dissatisfied with the level of knowledge and skill which the pupils were acquiring in home economics. Parents commented that home economics had not changed since they were in the program even though the role of the family in society had changed considerably.

The above evidence precipitated a keen determination to find a new approach to home economics. The schools wanted to prepare young men and women for an increasingly important role in the world of work as well as in the home. This determination led the staff to see that many of the concepts and generalizations which form the major portion of the body of knowledge in home economics were just as applicable to the world of work as to the family setting.

For example, the principles of child care, whether applied to the child in a day care center or to the child at home, remain the same; the principles of sanitation, whether applied to industry or to the home, are the same. By relating these concepts to industry, the students' horizons are broadened; and they do not feel that teachers are being critical of their personal lives.

As a result of the recognition of the need of change, the Cincinnati Public Schools began the development of a career orientation program. Textbooks and teachers' manuals were written and four schools were chosen to field test the materials during the 1969-70 school year. By the end of the second year of development, the staff felt confident that the program was worth further refinement but realized that additional resources were needed to achieve the goals. At this time, a meeting between McKnight Publishing Company and the

Cincinnati school system took place. Thus began a most unusual relationship whereby a publishing company and a school system agreed to work together to further develop a set of curriculum materials.

McKnight Publishing Company had the resources to bring together home economics teacher educators, city and state supervisors, and home economics teachers from across the nation to take part in the testing and planning of the program. Other specialists, including psychologists, audiovisual experts, and writers, contributed in the preparation of the **Exploring Careers in Child Care** program. This endeavor afforded the students in Cincinnati and across the nation a well-planned career development program that would have been impossible without such resources.

Although change is sometimes uncomfortable, home economics must be changed if men and women are to be prepared for the multiple roles they are to face in the future. **Exploring Careers in Child Care** provides a curriculum approach which gives students a general knowledge of child development and allows them to explore the many human work activities that take place in the child care environments.

The curriculum begins at the perception stage of learning by presenting the concepts, processes, and environments of child development. The core of the book provides simulations that help students analyze the concepts and processes in various environments which use child care knowledge and skills. It provides a core of experiences around which all future educational and occupational goals revolve. The concluding sections help students apply the concepts and processes to specific environments so they can plan their future more wisely.

In the past, the schools have done little to prepare students during their junior high school years to make wise decisions concerning the high school curriculum they will follow and the career goals which they wish to set for themselves. Yet, the students must make curriculum choices at the end of junior high school. Because there is a close relationship between education and careers, it seems evident that when students choose a high school curriculum, they are making both an educational and a career decision.

If schools are to improve the quality of life, they must prepare students to make decisions that will meet their personal needs and the needs of society. The **Exploring Careers in Child Care** program provides students with the knowledge and experience that will prepare them to make wise educational and career choices.

Marilyn Kay McFarland
Home Economics Instructional Consultant
Cincinnati Public Schools

Preface

You are about to be involved in a unique home economics program. **Exploring Careers in Child Care** will provide you with the opportunity to acquire the knowledge and skills needed to understand children's needs. During your studies, you will explore the child care environments of education, protection, and health care. You will experience the knowledge and skills used by workers in these environments as they help children grow and develop.

In each environment you will perform the human work activities used to operate enterprises as well as families. You will develop skills in these work activities:

- Researching
- Developing
- Preparing to Provide Services or Produce Products
- Providing Services or Producing Products
- Selling Services or Producing Products
- Controlling the System

This program provides information about the world of work that will help you in your daily life. The knowledge you gain can be used to make decisions in planning your career. You may use your understanding of work activities to become a wiser consumer of child care products or services. The skills and knowledge learned may also be used in your role as a family member — to make decisions, plan work to be done, and carry out individual responsibility. The knowledge and skills from **Exploring Careers in Child Care** are yours. It is up to you to use them in a way that fits your needs and personal goals.

Exploring Careers in Child Care is a complete program that includes a textbook, Activity Manual, Teacher's Guide, supplementary tests, instructional aids, and equipment. The program has been designed by professional educators, tested in selected schools across the nation, and revised to increase learning. The textbook explains concepts and will introduce you to cognitive information needed to perform the activities. The classroom activities reinforce the major concepts by giving you an opportunity to practice and perform skills and use your knowledge gained from the program. During activities you will experience the psychomotor activity that will help you draw your own affective conclusions. The Teacher's Guide contains the information necessary for the teacher's preparation and management of the educational environment for maximum learning.

The goal of the program is knowledge of the child care environments and human work activities performed within those environments. You will use your child care knowledge and skills to make career decisions, consumer decisions, and family decisions. By using your knowledge, you will be free to develop your potential in the direction that meets your personal needs.

Acknowledgments

Many people have contributed to the development of the **Exploring Careers in Child Care** program through field testing, consultation with writers, and review of the materials. We wish to acknowledge their contribution to this unique curriculum program. We also appreciate the cooperation of the many individuals and organizations who supplied illustrative materials for this publication.

Field Test Personnel

Instructional Consultant
Marilyn Kay McFarland

Coordinator
Marialyce Knoll

Public Schools
Cincinnati Field Tests

FIRST AND SECOND EDITIONS

Field Test Teachers

Betty Fultz
Marialyce Knoll
Sandra Dannemiller Graman
Scharleen Graham
Mary Johnson

Mary Geldreich
Maryellen Haas
Carol Schwindt
Alicia Kelly

Judy Kunz
Florence Bullis
Georgia Farley
Carol Rielage

THIRD EDITION

Field Test Teachers

Mary Johnson   Alicia Kelly

National Field Test

FOURTH EDITION

Field Test Teachers

Arizona

COORDINATOR
Barbara Border

TEACHER
Suzanne Aiton
Julia Delsid
Adrienne DeMinor

Kathy George
Ginger Guendelsberger
Mary Hardin
Rose Mary Hess

Patsy Hill
Sally Horcasitas
Marcia Koblinski
Karen Lattin
Marybeth Mason
Rachel Moreno
Thelma Shaw
Florence Weeks

Illinois

COORDINATOR
Vesta Morgan

TEACHER
Jackie Allen
Eloise Barber
Mary Ann Braden
Audrie Christensen
Brenda Butman
Nancy Colbert
Becky Duckworth
Della Frahm
Soneeta Grogan
Anna May Hance
Catherine Hasenmyer
June Haug
Adelia Inman
Janice Kalvaitis
Kay Kimmel
Joyce Kirkpatrick
Janet Lubbers
Nan Munsey
Jan Prince
Carolyn Rockabrand
Elda Ruckrigel
Carolyn Saxe
Marilyn Schroeder
Dorothy Smith
Phyllis Titus
Ocean Weaver
Cecilia H. Whaley

Indiana

COORDINATOR
Dr. Phyllis Lowe

(assisted by Jean Bush)

TEACHER
Helen Aldridge
Kathleen Anderson
Winifred Berryman
Mary E. Bland
Geraldine Carpenter
Anna Davenport
Phyllis Fischer
Suzanne Geringer
Carol Guess
Beverly Hudson
Peggy Jolly
Annette LaRowe
Delores Manning
Karen Martindill
Shirley Ann Moore
Colleen Shook
Faith Stryker
Algernon Weatherspoon
Janet Welch

Massachusetts

COORDINATOR
Martha Duckett

TEACHER
Theresa Bakunas
Virginia Barry
Sally Bear
Avis Child
Margaret Dempsey
Margaret Favreau
Mary Lou Hart
Florence Johnson
Shirley Jones

Catherine Lewis
Martha Mattox
Mary E. Meehan
Marilyn Timmons
Evelyn Touhey
Marian Westbrook

New Orleans

COORDINATOR
Mary Catherine Eble

TEACHER
Hattie F. Bennett
Agatha R. Jones
Ray D. Minor
Rita W. Montgomery
Catherine A. Plemmons
Iola F. Winfield

New York City

COORDINATOR
Marie Daspro

TEACHER
Kathleen Denneen
Lila Gordon
Dorothy Perkins
Edith Silberman

Wichita, Kansas

COORDINATOR
Helen Frieze

TEACHER
Judy David
Loretta Knutson
Doris Mayhew
Janet Meyer
Bonnie Rhoads
Joan Stafford
Ann Studer

Consultants and Reviewers

Beugen, Joan
Executive Vice President
The Creative Establishment

Callis, Bruce
Personnel Office
State Farm Insurance Company

Cope, Cecil
Legal Department
Illinois Agricultural Association

Cortese, Carl J., D. P. M.
Hadden Foot Clinic

Crown, Marjorie
State of Illinois, Department of Children and
Family Services

Davis, Howard
Supervisor of Curriculum
McLean County Unit 5 School District

Doughty, Dr. William
Baby Fold

Eggers, Dr. Sharon
Psychologist

Gailey Eye Clinic Ltd.

Hage, Maxine
Registered Nurse

Hammitt, Rev. Wm. A.
Baby Fold

Henderson, William, M.D.
Henderson Obstetrics Clinic

James, Dr. Jeanne
Home Economics Department
Illinois State University

Jenson, Dr. Carl
　Psychology Department
　Illinois Wesleyan University

Johnson, Carol
　Director
　La Petite Academy of Bloomington-Normal

Johnson, Dr. James
　Psychology Department
　Illinois State University

Kimbrell, Mary Ellen
　Registered Nurse

Kniery, James
　State of Illinois, Department of Children
　and Family Services

Lilly, Lois
　Elementary Education Department
　Illinois State University

Lux, Michael I.
　Architect
　Evans Associates

Madore, Dr. Normand
　Elementary Education Department
　Illinois State University

Martin, Richard, D.D.S.
　Pedodontist

Nelson, Emily
　Supervisor
　La Petite Academy

Nofziger, Libby
　Registered Nurse

Rouse-Eastin, David L.
　Psychologist
　Allied Agencies

Turner, Mary Ann
　Registered Nurse

Waldman, Marvin, D.P.M.
　Hadden Foot Clinic

Williams, Mary
　State of Illinois, Department of Children
　and Family Services

Sources of Illustration

American Airlines
American Foundation for the Blind
American President Lines
AMF Wheel Goods
　A Division of AMF Inc.
AT&T Photo Service
Atomics International
Ball State University
　Photographic Laboratory
　Photo by Michael Kerper
Baltimore City Health Department
BSA Photo by
　Watson Explorer Specialty Post
Chas. Pfizer & Company, Inc.
Chicago Board of Health
Chicago Daily News
Chicago Tribune
The Columbus Area Chamber of Commerce
Creative Playthings
The DuPont Company
E. I. duPont de Nemoure & Company, Inc.
Eastman Kodak Company
Evenflo Company
　A Division of Questor
Family Photography
　Campbell, Mrs. Jan
　Collie, Mrs. Jean
　Carr, Mrs. Betsy
　Dennison, Mrs. Ann
　Gordon, Mrs. Carolyn
　Martin, Mrs. Sharon
　McCracken, Mrs. Carol
　Polacek, Mrs. Marsha
　Shea, Mrs. Susie
　Taylor, Mrs. Barbara
　Wilmot, Mrs. Barbara

Fields, LeRoy
Ford Motor Company
　Educational Affairs Department
Gilbert Surgical and Medical Supplies, Inc.
Humiston, Leslie A.
International Business Machines
Johns-Manville Corporation
Kellog Company
Kendall Company
Los Angeles County Health Department
Masonite Corporation
McCabe-Powers Body Company
McCall's Patterns
Miami-Dade Junior College
Miami Herald Publishing Company
Motorola, Inc.
Nabisco Company
National Cotton Council
Northrop Corporation
Pacific Gas and Electric Company News Bureau
Photographers
　LePine, Jennifer
　Mowery, James
　Phillips, Todd
The Proctor & Gamble Company
Professional Photographers of America
The Rowland Company, Inc.
Sambo's Restaurant, Inc.
Selmer
　A Division of Magnavox
Towson State College
　Boyd, Ellsworth
UAW Solidarity
WMAR TV, Baltimore, Maryland
UNICEF Photo
Wirebound Box Manufacturers Association

Table of Contents

Exploring Human Needs

Who are you ? ? ? ? ? ? ? ?? ? ? ?
How would you answer that question? You could give your name or your nationality. If you were an adult, you might identify yourself by your occupation. No matter who you are, where you live, or how old you are, you can give the same answer as everyone else in this world by replying, "I am a human being!"

Just think about that. You share your humanness with people in every nation, in every corner of the globe. You belong to the human race. Although you have arms, legs, eyes, hair, teeth, and brains much like everyone else, you share something in common with other people that is just as important. You share **human needs.**

All people have the same needs. To explore and understand these needs, you do not have to travel to distant lands to study many different people. When you look at yourself, you are looking at a person whose needs are typical of everyone's needs. As you explore human needs in this course, you are going to discover some things about yourself and the rest of the human race that you did not know before!

PHYSICAL NEEDS

It had been snowing all day. The big, white flakes sugar-coated the bare trees and hills, and the air was snapping crisp. It was perfect weather for sledding. When school ended for the day,

1

all of Mary's friends got their sleds. None of them loved sledding as much as Mary did, but she did not join them. Mary had something else on her mind. She was thinking of **food** — sandwiches, apples, and steaming hot cocoa. Mary was VERY hungry: She ran right past those beautiful, snow-covered hills and did not stop until she reached the kitchen door at home.

The most basic human need is **physical,** a fact Mary recognized when she realized how hungry she was. Human physical need for food, air, clothing, and shelter begins at birth and continues all through life. When physical needs are being satisfied, not much thought is given to them. However, late in the afternoon when a person's stomach is empty and the smell of dinner cooking drifts out of the kitchen, all thoughts turn to food. Wanting physical needs satisfied is a never-ending desire and is one of the human traits.

The human need for **protection** is both a physical and an emotional need. Everyone wants to feel protected from harm, fear, and disorder. Because infants are afraid of falling, adults hold them securely. This offers physical protection. Children are sometimes afraid of the dark and may hide under their bed covers in a dark bedroom. Adults offer them emotional security when they assure them of their safety. Children should never be frightened for the sake of fun. This disturbs their feeling of emotional security and protection. In addition, adults protect children physically by providing food, shelter, and clothing.

SOCIAL-EMOTIONAL NEEDS

Robinson Crusoe was a sailor whose ship sank during a storm. He was the only one saved from drowning when he was washed up on the shore of a little island. He was all alone there, but he was so busy meeting his physical needs that he did not have time to think about loneliness. He built a shelter and learned how to locate food and fresh water. After he satisfied these needs, Crusoe became aware of other

The basic needs of every human being begin at birth and continue all through life.

Parents help meet the physical needs of their children by protecting them with food, shelter, and clothing.

needs. He needed companionship and wanted to share his thoughts with other people. He wanted to work at something useful and be recognized for his achievements, but there was no one with whom to share his life. When he finally found another human being on the island, he found great satisfaction in the new companionship.

You are no different than Robinson Crusoe. You have the same social and emotional needs that he had. You want to give and receive love. You want a feeling of belonging in your social environment. You want that good feeling of knowing that you are doing worthwhile things in life and are being recognized for your efforts by your family and friends. When these needs are not met, you may become very unhappy and lose confidence in yourself.

Parents often hold and touch their infants and children to show their love. Being held and hugged makes children feel warm and secure. As children grow up, parents encourage them to perform different tasks, such as tie their shoes, run errands, play independently, care for a pet, or handle a newspaper route. In these ways, children build a sense of confidence and independence. Think about yourself. Is receiving and giving love important to you? Do you have a need to do things for yourself and to have your efforts appreciated?

BECOMING YOURSELF

Tom and Alice were twins. During their 14 years of life, they had wanted for very few things. Both had been given good food, beautiful clothing, and a fine home. They had many friends. There was only one thing wrong in their lives. Tom and Alice were very bored.

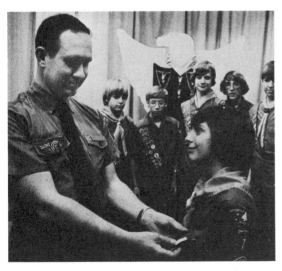

Receiving the recognition of your friends and neighbors can help fulfill the need for love and feeling of belonging.

Parents involve their children in activities that will help them understand how to meet their own needs some day.

At first our needs are met by others.

As we grow, we learn how to meet some of our own needs.

As we develop our skills, we set goals and then work to achieve them.

Although we never really stop becoming, we can at least reach many of our goals and experience the freedom of being ourselves.

"We really are lucky," said Alice. "There are so many people who haven't had the things we just take for granted. I don't understand why we aren't happy."

"I think we need to **do something worthwhile**," said Tom. "My teacher says everyone needs to become all they can be as human beings."

"Maybe you are right," said Alice. "Think about people like President Abraham Lincoln or ex-Prime Minister of Israel, Golda Meir. Think about the singer Barbra Streisand, and the tennis champion Billie Jean King, and the businessman Henry Ford. They're famous for one reason. They set goals and worked toward them. They've done something worthwhile. I remember reading that Lincoln once said, 'I will prepare myself; my chance will come.' We should get ready for our chance, too," said Alice.

"I have a goal. I want to become as good a father someday as Dad is," said Tom. "I think that's an important goal."

"I'm interested in government," said Alice. "I might set becoming a senator in Congress as my goal. I'm free to be whatever I can be."

You, too, are free to become YOU. As a human being, you hold great promise of becoming whatever you have the ability and desire to become. There is a need within you to fulfill that promise. Only you can hold yourself back from reaching that fulfillment. It is up to you to say YES TO LIFE and seek its experiences and investigate its responsibilities.

Have you ever read any books by Elmer Twiddle Dee? Of course not. Elmer Twiddle Dee is the writer who gave up before he fulfilled the promise he showed as a writer. Will you fulfill the promise of what you can become? **Will you become all you can be?**

THE FAMILY AND THE ENTERPRISE

Human needs are met by (1) families and (2) enterprises (organizations and businesses that produce products and services). Families provide for **physical** needs by giving children good food, clothing, and shelter and by protecting them from harm. Enterprises provide for physical needs by making clothing in factories or growing food on

Families provide an environment to protect, educate, and maintain the health of children.

farms. Families provide for **social-emotional** needs by giving family members love and encouragement and allowing them the independence they need to build confidence in themselves. Many organizations, such as school, church, and the Girl Scouts and Boy Scouts, also provide opportunities that can answer the need for achievement and self-esteem (a feeling of worth).

Family and enterprises provide a sound basis for your development as an individual when they meet your physical and social-emotional needs. This is why they are so important during the growing stages of infancy, childhood, teen-age years, young adulthood, and adulthood. They cannot, however, meet your need to become **you.** Only you can fill that need, and that is by setting personal goals in life and working toward them. •

In a community, enterprises help families by providing special products and services to meet children's needs.

REVIEWING YOUR VOCABULARY

nationality
identify
occupation
humanness
human needs
explore
physical needs
traits
protection
disorder
assurance
social-emotional needs
companionship
recognized
achievement

environment
confidence
secure
independence
appreciated
goals
ability
fulfill
investigate
possibilities
enterprises
encouragement
self-fulfillment
development

INCREASING YOUR PERCEPTION

1. Explain how you are like everyone else in this world.
2. Identify your needs for physical care and protection.
3. How do you satisfy your need for love and belonging?
4. How can you find out what your interests are and what you are capable of becoming?
5. What are your goals concerning family, friends, career, and leisure time activities?
6. How does the family and the enterprise work together to meet the needs of children?

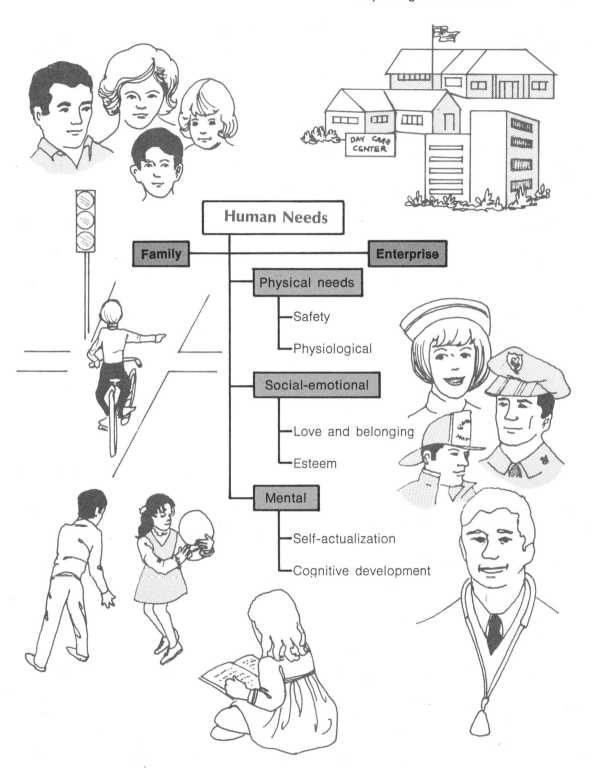

Human Needs

Family — **Enterprise**

Physical needs
- Safety
- Physiological

Social-emotional
- Love and belonging
- Esteem

Mental
- Self-actualization
- Cognitive development

Exploring Personal Needs

Ken and Mary are brother and sister. Both of them are good students and want to be important people someday. Ken's abilities and interests are in science. He wants to become a doctor. Mary is interested in government. She wants to become a city planner. Ken and Mary each have goals to reach. Their individual goals represent a personal need that must be fulfilled.

INFANCY

CHILDHOOD

TEEN-AGER

YOUNG ADULT

ADULT

Each of us has the same needs in life, but we satisfy our needs in different ways.

Ken and Mary share the same human need — the need for **self-fufillment.** Each of them must reach a different goal before they can satisfy their personal need for self-fulfillment. All human beings are different in the ways they meet their personal needs. This difference is what makes each person an **individual.** Meeting personal needs differently is what causes one person to be a doctor and another a city planner.

Successfully meeting human needs in one's own individual way is the goal of each person. As people achieve this goal, they are in the process of **becoming** (or growing toward) whatever they can be as human beings. There are **five main stages** of becoming:

- Infancy
- Childhood
- Teen-ager
- Young adult
- Adult

In each stage, even infancy, people show that they are individuals in the ways they **think; use their bodies; care** about people, places, and things; and **live their personal lives.** A look at each of these separately will help you learn more about yourself and others.

THINKING

Awareness is the key to using your ability to think and learn.

In 1797, three hunters in France captured a strange, humanlike creature in the woods. It was covered with dirt and scars and had long, matted hair. The "creature" turned out to be a boy about 11 years old. How he happened to be living in the forest and how long he had been there, no one knew. The boy did not eat cooked food and could not speak any form of human language. He could not understand the simplest words. The boy had learned how to think and live like an animal.

A doctor attempted to educate the strange boy, but had only limited success. "Victor, the Wolf Boy," as he was called, could not think or learn like a human being. He was not **aware** of human ways. He could not **understand** how to use a bed, a drinking cup, or words. Victor had learned to use animal knowledge to take care of his physical needs. He did not **value** the knowledge that the doctor tried to teach him. Victor could not think or act like a human being. Victor remained more animal than human the rest of his life.

What do you think really made Victor so different from other human beings? The answer is simple. Victor was not **aware** that he was a member of the human family. He needed to be aware of this fact before he could begin thinking and acting like a human. Awareness is essential when **mental** ability is to be used.

The first step in thinking, then, is **being aware** that information is useful in helping meet personal needs. All people differ in their amount of awareness. For instance, you might be very aware that the names and numbers listed in the sports page of the newspaper are the daily baseball scores of many teams. If you did not know that baseball was a game, then of how much **value** would these numbers be to you?

This symbol has value to those that are aware of its meaning.

If you found this symbol ⊗ on the side of a house, would you be **aware of the value of this information?** It was a sign that hobos (idle wanderers) used many years ago to show that the owners of the house would give hobos free food. Were you aware of the meaning of this symbol?

The second step in thinking is that of **understanding.** A person might be aware of information but not understand it. People differ in the way they understand. An infant may understand that a gentle hug means love. If squeezed too hard, the infant may not understand. Very difficult puzzles can be worked quickly by some people who understand them. Others do not understand how to solve these puzzles. Some people understand how to care for children and some do not.

When an infant cries, are you aware of its needs? Do you understand what to do? What **value** do you place on an infant's message of distress? Do you care?

The third step in thinking is to **use knowledge.** Everyone uses knowledge differently.

Bob and Sue both went to school to learn about cooking and dietetics (nutrition). Bob decided to use his knowledge by becoming a chef. He eventually became the head chef in a large restaurant. Sue used her knowledge as a hospital dietitian and supervised the preparation of hundreds of meals every day.

Bob and Sue had basically the same knowledge, but used it in different ways. There are many different careers because people can use their knowledge differently. How will you use the knowledge you gain in this course about children?

As people become more mature (grown up), they begin to **become aware** that knowledge is used to take care of their personal needs and the needs of other people. The following items were developed to satisfy human needs. **Are you aware of the knowledge** that was needed and used to develop these items? Are you aware of any human needs that are not being satisfied today? What knowledge will be used to meet the personal needs of people in the future and who are the people that will meet those needs? Will you have the knowledge to satisfy your personal needs? Will you help other people with your knowledge?

Although Helen Keller could not see or hear, she developed her other senses of taste, touch, and feeling and acquired the skills and knowledge that would satisfy her needs.

USING OUR BODIES

Helen Keller could not see or hear. Her weakness in those two **senses** made her different from other people. To make up for having no sight and hearing, Helen developed her other senses of **touch, smell, and taste.** Although she could not see or hear, she could smell, taste, and feel things others could not. Her strength in these senses made her different from other people. She used those senses to develop personal skills and acquire knowledge that would satisfy her needs.

The five human senses are a very important part of your body. It is **through your senses that you receive information and** **knowledge** from the world around you. How Helen Keller used her senses made her different from other people. Your ability to use your senses will be different from others, too.

Each person is different because each has different physical skills. Perhaps you admire someone who is physically attractive, physically strong, or physically agile and quick. You want to be like that person. What you must realize is that you are not another person. You are yourself. You must know and understand your own physical abilities and limitations. If you become aware of your physical self, then you can begin using and improving physical abilities to achieve your personal goals.

Jim stepped up to the batter's box. He hated baseball. He was coordinated well enough, but the **big muscles** in his arms did not seem to swing the bat at the right moment. Jim looked at his friend Dan. "That guy can hit more home runs than anyone in the league," Jim thought. As usual, Jim struck out. As usual, Dan hit a home run. Later that day, Jim showed Dan the new ring he had made in a little shop in his basement. Dan shook his head in admiration. "Gee," Dan thought, "I wish I could make a ring like that. The **small muscles** in my hands just aren't developed like Jim's."

Both Jim and Dan could use their body muscles in skillful, but different ways. Like Jim and Dan, children use their bodies differently. They first learn to use the big muscles in their legs and arms. Some children are very strong and learn to use their arms and legs well. Others take longer to develop their large muscles. The small muscles in children's hands and fingers begin to develop later. A child with strong big muscles may have weak small muscles while a child with well-developed small muscles may not use his large muscles as well. All children are different in the way they make use of their physical abilities.

Each individual must become aware of and understand his or her physical abilities and limitations.

WHO CARES?

How much you **value** different things is shown by your attitudes. In the long run, your success or failure may depend more on attitude and value than on ability alone. The following story is about the make-believe attitudes and values of three different horses. Which attitude of these horses is most like yours? What does Dan, Breeze, and Dart each care about?

THE LONG RUN
by Ken Alvey

There once was a race horse named Dan
Who lost every race that he ran.
He said, "I'm the best!
No, not of the rest,
But the best I can be, I am!"

There once was a race horse named Breeze
Who won when he could win with ease.
He said, "I could win
Each race that I'm in,
But why run so hard that I wheeze?"

There once was a race horse named Dart
Who won every race he would start.
He said, "I'm the best!
Make glue of the rest!
I'm too fast, too good, and too smart!"

These three horses raced in the West.
Half through it, Breeze slowed down to rest.
Dart looked back to jeer,
Tripped and fell on his ear,
And Dan, who was worst, finished best!

How much people **care** accounts for one of the big differences in the way they meet their needs. If a person cares, he or she will probably meet a particular need in a much better way than someone who does not care. All people need personal recognition. A kind word of praise or a small award shows that other people care also. People have probably shown that they care about you. Have you ever shown that you care about someone?

It is very important for some people to belong to a certain social group. Other people are indifferent as to whether a group accepts them. Some people have a great need for self-respect, and they have a sense of responsibility to themselves and others. Perhaps you know a person who does not really care about those things, but does care about something else. What do you really care about?

Caring enough to practice swimming everyday helped Linda win the race.

PERSONAL GOALS

People differ in mental ability, attitudes, and the way they can use their bodies. These differences can be seen clearly in the personal goals people set for themselves. Study the following examples of Bill, Peggy, Betty, and Jack. Each one wants something unique (special) in life. Each one has different personal goals.

For Bill, the most important thing in life is his **family.** He earns a good living as a construction worker, but his main goal in life is to be a successful family member.

Peggy loves her **friends.** The more friends she has, the happier she becomes. Peggy has little trouble making new friends because she is kind and generous.

Betty's main interest in life is her **career** as a buyer of children's clothes for a large department store. She is not married, but has little time for friends. Betty is very happy, for she is meeting her need for a career.

Jack is a man of **leisure.** A self-employed artist, Jack works just as little as possible. He is not lazy. He simply values having leisure time for his main interests — fishing, hiking, and boating. Jack knows Betty and cannot understand her attitude toward work. He can't understand how anyone could be that interested in a career.

Have you found your own personal goals? Are you more like Jack than Betty? Do you value friends above all else? Is family the most important thing to you? There is no right answer. You are different from others and have a right to be yourself. You differ in the way you meet your needs and become yourself. To be successful, you must determine your goals and then care enough to reach them. In doing so, you will become a very special individual who is different from everyone else in the whole world.

REVIEWING YOUR VOCABULARY

personal need	adult	senses
individual	awareness	agile
becoming	value	recognition
infancy	symbol	responsibility
childhood	dietetics	unique
teen-ager	mature	career
young adult		

INCREASING YOUR PERCEPTION

1. Explain how you are different in each stage of human development from everyone else in the whole world.

2. Identify and explain the four steps in the process of thinking.

3. Give examples of how people can use their bodies differently.

4. How do your values cause you to be different from others that you know?

5. What personal goal seems most important to you?

6. What things do you do better than others you know?

7. What things do others do better than you?

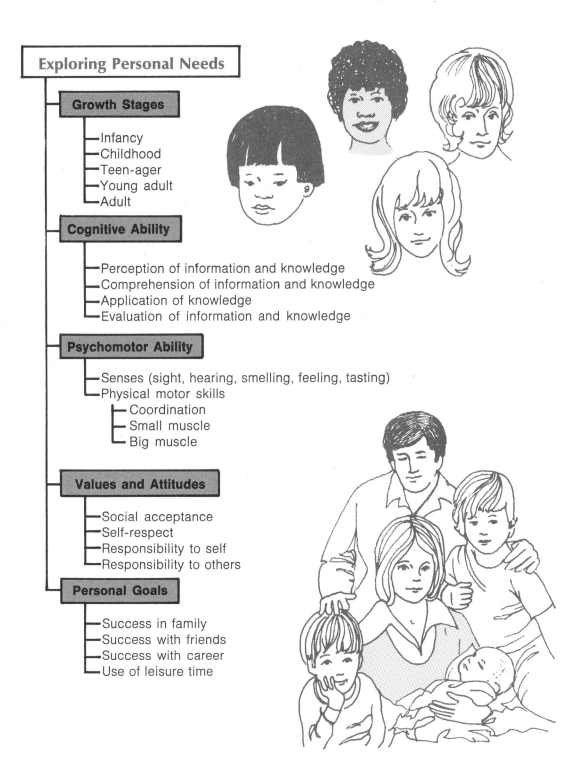

Exploring Personal Needs

Growth Stages
- Infancy
- Childhood
- Teen-ager
- Young adult
- Adult

Cognitive Ability
- Perception of information and knowledge
- Comprehension of information and knowledge
- Application of knowledge
- Evaluation of information and knowledge

Psychomotor Ability
- Senses (sight, hearing, smelling, feeling, tasting)
- Physical motor skills
  - Coordination
  - Small muscle
  - Big muscle

Values and Attitudes
- Social acceptance
- Self-respect
- Responsibility to self
- Responsibility to others

Personal Goals
- Success in family
- Success with friends
- Success with career
- Use of leisure time

Living in the Community

On a very cold, snowy day a long time ago, Momma and Papa Ugglug and their two children sat shivering in their cave. Neither the animal skins that they wore nor the little fire they had built kept them warm in their damp, dark home. The Ugglugs were also hungry, but there was no food. Papa Ugglug was a poor hunter in spite of the fine spears and clubs that he made. A visit from some neighbors would have been welcome at such an unhappy time, but no other families lived nearby.

A wild animal growled outside the entrance of the cave. Papa Ugglug moved closer to his little family. He wondered what would become of his wife and children if something happened to him. Even with him there, life was not very good. Momma Ugglug spent long hours making crude clothing from the stiff skins of animals, cooking over a hot fire, and making sure the children were not harmed by some intruding beast. Papa Ugglug roamed all day searching for food and usually found very little. They all feared illness, for they knew no way to treat an illness. Because the cave was so dirty and damp, the children were often sick.

The animal growled again. Papa Ugglug held his spear in readiness. His son watched. The little boy was already learning how to be a hunter. He knew how to follow animal tracks, throw his little spear, and build a fire. Momma Ugglug had taught her daughter to sew and cook. What else was there to learn in their lonely, difficult world? The Ugglugs did not like their world, but what other kind was there?

The cold, snowy days finally ended. In the spring, Papa Ugglug went on a long hunting trip. He returned very excited. He had found a number of families much like his own who were unhappy with their lives. They had decided to come together as a group.

The new chief formed the men and women into special groups. The best hunters would supply the meat. The best farmers would grow the food. The best builders would make huts. The best weavers would make the clothes. Others would entertain with songs and stories. Papa Ugglug was to be a tool- and spear-maker. The children could learn about many things from different members of the group. It would be a much better life. The Ugglugs left their lonely cave. They would never live alone again.

Human beings have found that living together in **communities** resulted in a much better life for both children and adults. Adults are concerned with a better life for children for a very good reason. Children are the future of the human race. If their needs for protection, health, and education are not met during the growing years, children may not develop into productive adults.

The family is still the environment (surroundings) where most children's needs are met. The family meets human needs through **protection, health,** and **education.** The Ugglugs did this as best they could. Today most families try to meet their needs just as the Ugglugs tried to meet theirs. Unlike the Ugglugs, however, they have **enterprises** that help them meet these needs. An enterprise is a group of people working together to produce products or services. A school, such as the one you attend, is an enterprise. Hospitals, clothing factories, farms, and toy stores are also enterprises. These enterprises, among others, help the family meet the needs of children in the community.

Families and enterprises have learned a great deal since the time of the Ugglug family. They have learned that by working together and providing protection, health, and education, they can meet the needs of children.

PURPOSE

Families and enterprises meet children's needs by having a **purpose.** To have a purpose for doing something means there is a **goal** to be reached. For a family or enterprise to reach its purpose or goal, it must meet children's needs.

The purpose of a family is to create a proper environment for children. In this environment, children can be kept safe from harm, can grow healthy and strong, and can learn about themselves and the world in which they live. The family not only meets children's needs for a home, clothing, and proper food, but also provides them with love and security.

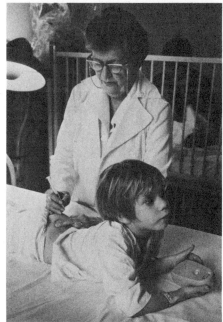

Families and enterprises exist to fulfill the basic needs of children for health, education, and protection.

One of the primary goals of families in a community is the care and protection of their children.

Parents provide playthings that not only stimulate a child's natural desire to touch and pull, but are safe to play with.

Each enterprise has a purpose, too. Kindergartens, elementary schools, nursery schools, and day care centers provide **education.** The child welfare agency and the adoption agency **protect** children. Hospitals, health care clinics, and programs for special children meet the **health** needs of children.

PROVIDING PROTECTION, HEALTH, AND EDUCATION

The big lamp on the tall table has a long tassle. To Sue, age eight months, it looks like a tail, and she wants more than anything else to pull that tail. The fact that the lamp could fall on her has never entered her mind. She crawls closer and reaches with her hand. "Oh, those silly bars!" Once again, the bars of her playpen have spoiled her fun. Sue's parents are providing for her **protection,** but Sue is not very happy about it. She sits down with a little bump and stares at the lamp cord. "That tail sure looks like it would be fun to pull."

To reach their goals, families provide protection such as playpens. Protecting children is also a job sometimes done by organizations outside the family.

Jerry and his mother lived alone in a little apartment above a store. When his mother became ill and was taken to the hospital for a long stay, Jerry had no one to care for him. The child welfare agency solved this problem. The people who worked for the agency found a temporary home for Jerry until his mother was well again. Jerry had a special need for this protective home because he is blind.

Families provide for the **health** of their children by serving three good meals a day. This helps children to develop healthy bodies. Because most families cannot grow all the food necessary for their meals, farmers raise livestock, grain, fruits, and vegetables. Grocery stores then sell the food to parents. If children become ill, hospitals or clinics provide treatment by using modern equipment and trained health care specialists.

Families also provide **education.** They help their children learn to do things for themselves. They encourage an interest in books and toys and provide new experiences for children. Children will find out more about the moon and the earth when they go to school, and about people and their ways. Nurseries, kindergartens, and elementary schools can provide learning experiences that family members cannot.

Parents know that nourishing foods will help keep their children healthy.

Since the process of education begins in the home, it is most important that parents take time to help children learn.

RESOURCES ARE INPUTS TO FAMILIES AND ENTERPRISES

Some Saturday when you have nothing better to do, why not build a rocket and go to the moon? That is a foolish idea, of course. Few people could build such a rocket, because they do not have the proper **resources**. To provide protection, health, and education for children, families and enterprises need resources, too. Below is a list of these resources called **inputs**.

KNOWLEDGE

Knowledge helps human beings to meet needs in new and better ways. Knowledge of protection has produced child welfare laws and agencies. Knowledge of health has resulted in modern medicine, clothing, and food. Knowledge of education has created schools to improve the minds of children.

PEOPLE

People work in the enterprises that provide protection, health, and education. People also are family members who create a living environment for children.

FINANCE

Finance is money. Enterprises borrow money to begin operations, so they can produce the products and services for protection, health, and education. Families work for enterprises in order to get the money necessary to provide for their children.

INDUSTRIAL RESOURCES

These resources are the materials and tools needed to provide protection, health, and education. A playpen is an industrial resource that protects a child. Medicine is an industrial resource that provides health. Books, school desks, and pencils are industrial resources that provide education.

UTILITY SERVICES

Communities provide sewage disposal plants that protect children from disease. Fuel, water, and electricity are utility services that meet children's health and educational needs. How healthy would you be during the winter without fuel? Would you be able to study in a school without electricity to provide lighting?

Momma and Papa Ugglug made a wise decision when they left their lonely cave. When they joined others, they found new and improved ways to provide for their needs. Children's needs are much better met in the community. Look closely at your own community. What enterprises meet the needs of children? Where are these enterprises located? Are more needed?

REVIEWING YOUR VOCABULARY

communities	temporary
health	treatment
protection	specialists
education	resources
productive	inputs
environment	knowledge
enterprise	finance
purpose	operations
goal	production
security	industrial resources
special children	utility service
organizations	

INCREASING YOUR PERCEPTION

1. Explain how living in a community has made life better for people and children.
2. Identify how the community can help families provide for children's health, education, and protection.
3. List all of the family members who care for children.

4. List all of the specialists in the community who care for children.

5. Identify the special resources used by families and enterprises to care for children.

6. Identify the special resources in your home or in your classroom that you could use to care for children.

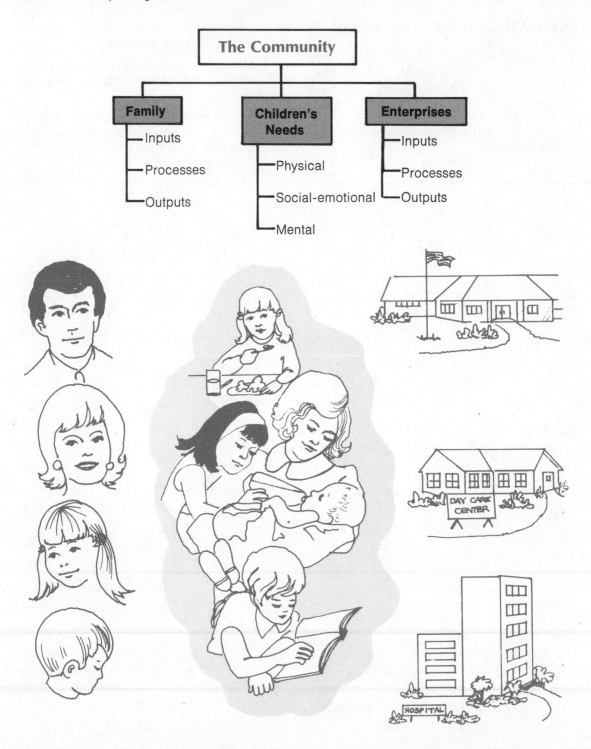

The Community

Family
— Inputs
— Processes
— Outputs

Children's Needs
— Physical
— Social-emotional
— Mental

Enterprises
— Inputs
— Processes
— Outputs

Caring for a Child's Daily Needs

Charles and Judy were going to be parents for the first time. They had been planning for the birth of their baby for several months. Judy had been visiting a special doctor called an **obstetrician** during her pregnancy. The obstetrician had given her a physical examination and a series of laboratory tests to find any health problems she might have. He had also put Judy on a diet that would supply her and the fetus (unborn child) with the necessary amounts of protein, vitamins, and minerals. Judy made frequent visits to the obstetrician where her weight and general health were carefully checked. During this busy and happy time, Charles and Judy also bought baby clothing, feeding supplies, and nursery furniture.

At last the baby was near birth. Charles took Judy to the hospital where they were met by the obstetrician who would deliver the child. A nurse helped Judy register and then saw that she was safely taken to her room. When it was time for the baby to be born, the doctor and several nurses assisted Judy. A medical secretary then recorded birth weight, length, and name of Charles and Judy's new daughter, Ann. The doctor filled out a birth certificate which Ann would need later on in life for entrance into school, marriage, or to get a passport to visit other countries. Lab technologists tested Ann's

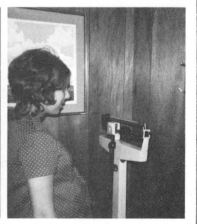

Planning to meet a child's needs begins long before birth. Proper diet and exercise keep the mother and unborn infant in good health. Products such as blankets, cribs, and baby feeding utensils must be ready before the baby is born.

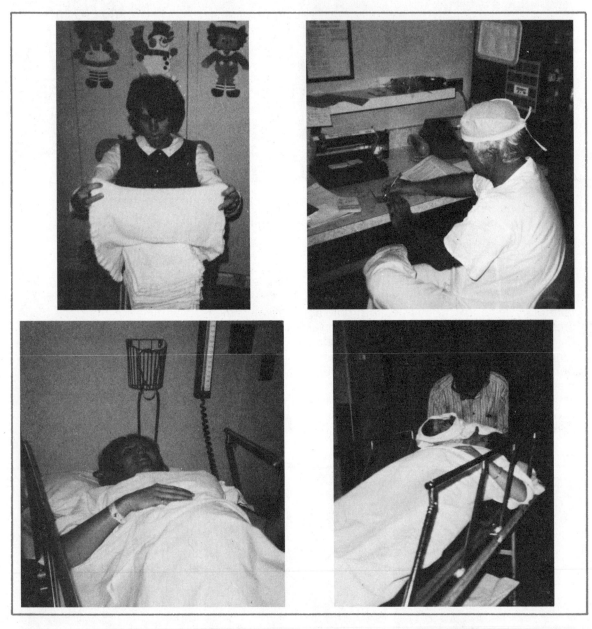

Everyone must prepare for a child's needs before and after childbirth.

urine for **phenylketonuria.** This is a disease that could cause mental retardation and is controlled by diet.

Charles was very nervous when he and his wife brought their newborn daughter home from the hospital. He knew his job as a construction worker, but he had never taken care of a baby in his life. He hoped that Judy knew what to do. Maybe she had learned something about infants during her career as a social worker at a child welfare agency. This new world of diapers, bottles, and feedings was pretty mysterious to him. Charles watched closely as Judy placed their daughter Ann in the newly purchased crib.

"Are you sure the sides of the crib are on tight?" asked Judy.

"Of course they are. I put the crib together myself," said Charles. "If I can construct buildings, I certainly can construct a crib."

"Well, it's important for little Ann to have a safe place to sleep. We don't want her to fall. Charles, what are you doing with that big, stuffed rabbit?"

"I'm going to put it in the crib with her."

"It's too big for a little baby, Charles. And it's got wire in its ears that could hurt Ann."

"I didn't think about that."

"We have to be aware of those kinds of dangers now," said Judy. "There are many things we must think about if we are to give our baby the kind of daily care she needs. We must be aware of Ann's health and education needs as well as her protection needs."

"How could she need education now?" asked Charles. "She can't even focus her eyes."

"Ann is already learning by just listening to the sounds of our voices. Someday she will start to say words. She'll learn to speak our language by listening to us. If we talk to her every day, she will learn to talk."

"I didn't know that. I guess I don't know much of anything about babies."

Judy laughed. "Don't worry, Charles. You'll learn a great deal about babies in the next year. The most important thing now is for us to **become aware** of our child's daily needs. Then we must learn what to do and how to do it. Adults must become aware that children need **protection, health care,** and **education** every day of their lives. You can't protect a baby one day and then forget about it the next day."

"It's like constructing a building," said Charles. "The plans have to be followed carefully every day."

"That's right," said Judy. "Children depend upon parents and that big system of enterprises that helps parents meet children's needs. That's what child care is all about — **meeting the daily needs** of children."

PROTECTION

As Ann began to grow, Charles found that protecting her was one of the most difficult jobs he had ever had. "Putting up that 20-story office building on 42nd street was a lot easier," he told Judy.

As the days and weeks passed, the new parents became even more aware of Ann's need for a safe area in which to play, sleep, and eat. The big rabbit with wire ears was put away. Toys safe for babies were given to Ann. She slept in a crib that was carefully constructed so she could not fall out. Her parents made sure it was placed away from heaters or drafty windows. Ann was never left alone in her high chair or during her bath. When she started to crawl around, Charles bought a playpen that kept her from reaching light cords and other dangerous objects.

Charles and Judy realized that they could also protect their daughter from **emotional** harm by giving her a lot of love. Their gentleness and attention made Ann a happy baby who knew that she was wanted and loved. When Judy sang to her at bedtime, her soft voice made Ann feel secure.

Once in a while Charles found himself wondering what would happen if he and Judy were not able to take care of the baby. Who would become responsible for the baby? Who would protect and educate their child, and who would care for her health?

"Don't you remember? I am making a career of being a social worker," Judy said. "The child welfare agency where I work protects hundreds of children every year

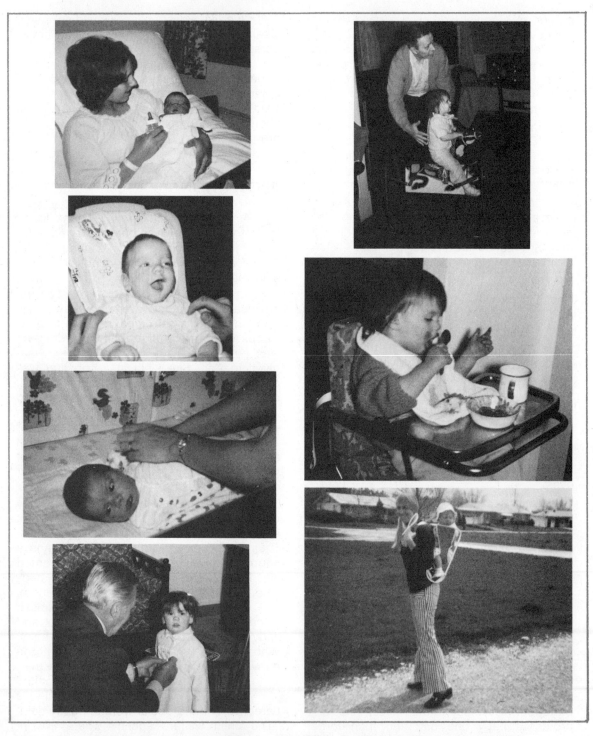

Parents become responsible for the child's health, protection, and education.

who have lost their parents or have parents who can't care for them. We find homes for such children and make sure they receive love and security."

"I thought you only helped special children who had physical or mental handicaps."

"Yes, that is my special work. Our agency protects those children in either special schools or institutions, but welfare agencies help all children who need protection."

"That means our government becomes responsible for the protection of children," said Charles. "And laws protect children from harm."

"Yes, and laws help people adopt homeless children."

"I feel better," said Charles. "It's good to know there's a system that helps parents protect their children. We have a big job and need all the help we can get."

HEALTH CARE

Charles and Judy were both healthy people who enjoyed swimming, tennis, and hiking. They wanted their daughter also to have good health so that she could enjoy life too. If she was to grow up strong and

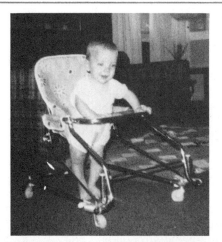

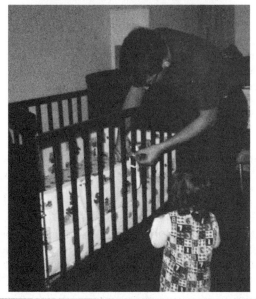

Enterprises and parents are responsible for protecting children.

Child welfare agencies protect children by placing them in good foster homes until qualified parents are prepared to adopt them.

happy, they realized that she must receive health care every day.

With the help of a **pediatrician** (a children's doctor), Charles and Judy learned what kind of daily diet, rest, and exercise Ann would need at different stages in her growth. They became aware of the signs of certain illnesses and how to care for Ann until she was well again. Charles and Judy made sure their daughter had frequent checkups with the pediatrician, Dr. Navarro.

"Through these examinations," Dr. Navarro told the couple, "I hope to prevent any serious illness by finding and treating small ones before they develop into big ones. I will examine Ann very carefully. If I find anything wrong, I will order either medicine or some other form of treatment to make her well. Also, by helping you to improve her health care at home, Ann should become a healthy adult."

Charles and Judy worked out a system at home. They cared for Ann by keeping her clean, well fed, and warm. They discovered that Ann needed milk about every three or four hours when she was a small baby. Charles often crawled out of his warm bed at three o'clock in the morning to give Ann her bottle. By age one, Ann's needs had changed. She then required only three meals a day with midmorning and afternoon snacks. Charles wondered just how Judy knew what kind of food was best for Ann.

One day Charles did the grocery shopping for Judy. She gave him a list of Ann's basic food needs, as suggested by Dr. Navarro. This was the list:

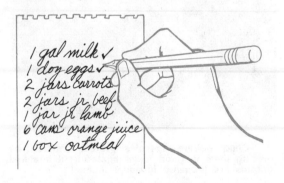

By giving Ann the right kind of food she needed every day, Charles and Judy were ensuring good health care for their daughter.

EDUCATION

Charles had always thought of education as a school's responsibility. He soon became aware that children's education begins in the home and continues every day of their lives, no matter where they are. As a baby, Ann often played with her fingers and toes and later with toys that her parents provided. She was learning to use her body. At first, Ann could only use her large muscles in her arms and legs as she played. She pushed, pulled, and hit. When older, Ann developed the little muscles in her hands and fingers. She could pinch, twist, and even draw a little.

Charles and Judy made sure that Ann had every opportunity to develop properly. They supplied her with toys and the freedom to grow at her own pace. They depended on enterprises to produce the many products, such as playpen, building blocks, and books that would help their child's development.

Ann's education was taking place, too. As a baby she needed an interesting environment of changing scenes, different sounds, and adult speech. These experiences stimulated her mind and encouraged mental growth. Hearing speech was very important for Ann's own speech development.

When she grew older, Ann wanted to learn more about herself and the world around her. As she asked questions and gained new knowledge about her world, her imagination developed. Ann used her imagination to act out things she experienced. A visit to the grocery store, for example, often resulted in "playing store" at home. She also used her imagination in drawing pictures, enjoying books, and playing with other children. Charles and Judy were aware of the experiences needed for their daughter's education and therefore created an

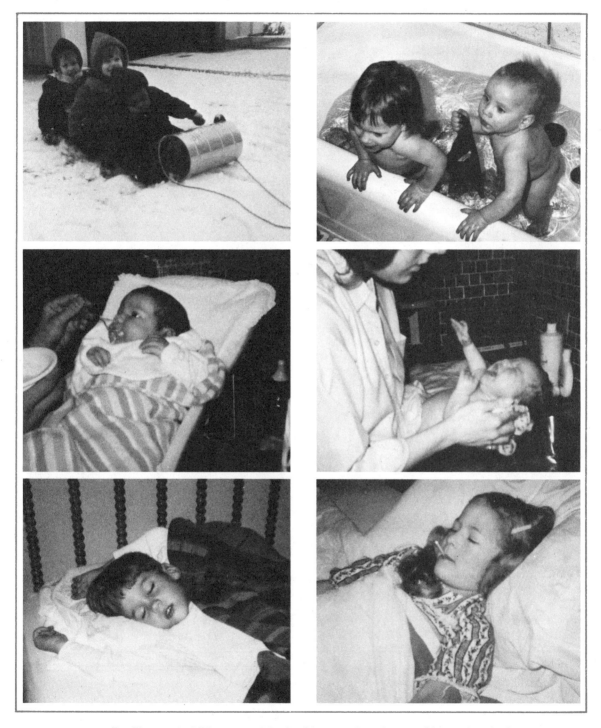

Families meet children's need for health care when they provide good sanitation, the proper amount of rest, nutritious foods, exercise, and loving care.

Educational needs of children are met when parents provide books, educational toys, and the opportunity to experiment, explore, and learn about their world.

environment where education could take place. Also, Ann attended a nursery school and kindergarten. Later she went to elementary school where formal learning took place.

As Ann becomes educated, she must decide how important her knowledge is and how she wants to use it. Ann may place higher value on her ability to play tennis than on her knowledge of reading. Or, she may decide to spend a great deal of time working on a science project rather than baking a pie. In making such decisions, Ann will learn about herself and her place in the world. Charles and Judy are aware that their daughter must be allowed the freedom to make her choices if she is to develop herself fully as a person.

PROVIDING GOODS AND SERVICES

Charles and Judy will spend about 18 years caring for Ann's daily needs. It is one of the most important things they will ever do, and they both realize their many responsibilities for her well-being. They will provide Ann with a great variety of services and products that will meet her daily needs.

Charles and Judy will be aided in their task by a **supportive system**. Charles could liken a supportive system to his work. During construction of a building, a network of iron beams supports the floors. In raising a child, a network of enterprises will support Charles and Judy by supplying them with child care products and services that will help protect and educate Ann and maintain her health. For example, the supportive system produces food which Judy prepares for Ann. It also produces books and records for her education. It provides parks where Charles can take Ann for exercise. Different and interesting environments will aid in her development as an individual.

Charles and Judy must decide what products and services best fill Ann's needs. They must then provide them. It is the responsibility of the supportive system to research, plan, and provide those products

and services that Charles and Judy need for their daughter. If the supportive system does not meet its responsibility, Ann's need for health, education, and protection may not be met and, as a result, she may not develop properly.

As you can see, neither parents nor the supportive system alone can totally meet the daily needs of children. It is only when they work together that children like Ann have the best chance to grow into happy, healthy adults.

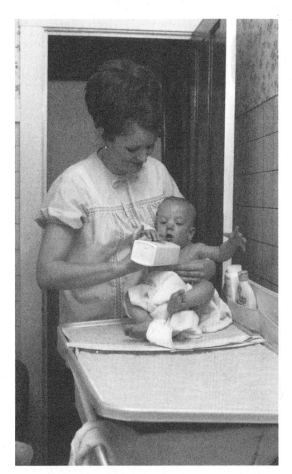

Parents use services and products provided by the supportive system to meet the daily needs of their children.

REVIEWING YOUR VOCABULARY

obstetrician
physical examination
laboratory tests
fetus
diet
proteins
vitamins
minerals
technologists
phenylketonuria
urine

retardation
handicaps
institutions
pediatrician
stimulated
mental growth
speech
 development
imagination
well-being
supportive system

INCREASING YOUR PERCEPTION

1. Identify examples of children's daily needs.

2. How do families help children meet their daily needs?

3. How do workers in the supportive system help children meet their daily needs?

4. List ways that you can help children meet their daily needs.

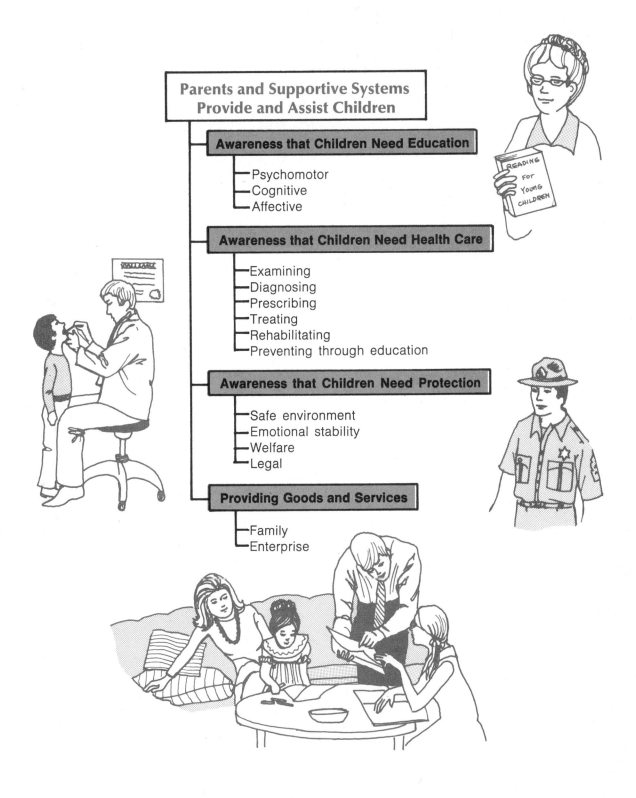

Parents and Supportive Systems Provide and Assist Children

Awareness that Children Need Education
- Psychomotor
- Cognitive
- Affective

READING FOR YOUNG CHILDREN

Awareness that Children Need Health Care
- Examining
- Diagnosing
- Prescribing
- Treating
- Rehabilitating
- Preventing through education

Awareness that Children Need Protection
- Safe environment
- Emotional stability
- Welfare
- Legal

Providing Goods and Services
- Family
- Enterprise

Communicating with Children

Father: "This is the third bad report card you've brought home. You are in big trouble! There will be NO more parties, dances or ANYTHING else until these grades improve. Now go to YOUR room!"

Billy: "But Dad, I can't —"

Father: "The conversation is over. LEAVE THE ROOM!"

Is that communication? No. It could hardly be called a conversation. Neither Billy nor his father are reaching one another. There is a block between them as real as a brick wall.

Father: "Billy, your report cards haven't been good lately. I really believe you can do better than this. What do you think?"

Billy: "Yes, I think so, too."

Father: "All right, let's sit down and see if we can find the problem and solve it. I know how you feel. I had this trouble when I was about your age."

That is communication. Ideas and information have been sent out and received. An understanding has been reached. Communication does not mean that people always agree with one another. It does mean that ideas are exchanged and each person at least listens to what the other person has to say.

Adults often find it difficult to communicate with each other. Communicating with children can be even MORE difficult. Their understanding of spoken or written language is very limited. They may only be able to understand simple ideas and suggestions. Adults, however, must be able to communicate with children, for that is the only way children can learn and grow.

If you enter a career in the child care field or become a parent, you must be able to communicate. Becoming skillful in communicating with children will also help you communicate with people your own age and older. Everyone must learn to break down those brick walls that prevent communication.

COMMUNICATING

Mary has been taking piano lessons for about three months. She has found it to be increasingly hard work and wants to quit.

Mother: "Stopping the lessons is your decision, Mary. But think how you love music. It gives you a great deal of

THE PROCESS OF COMMUNICATION INVOLVES:

1 Thinking of a message

2 Sending the message

3 Receiving the message

4 Understanding the message

5 Remembering the message

6 Responding to the message

satisfaction. Other people will enjoy listening to you."

Mary: "The lessons are boring. I'm not very good, either. I can hear a beautiful sound in my mind, but when I play it, it just sounds awful."

Mother: "I think you're being hard on yourself. You've only been taking lessons for three months. You'll improve in time. If you quit now, Mary, you'll never be good enough to get any real satisfaction out of playing the piano.

And others will be denied the satisfaction of listening to you. Please think about it before you make a decision."

Mary: "I will. It would be wonderful if I could learn to play well."

Mary has a wise mother. She knows how to communicate an idea. She realized that Mary received much satisfaction from music. That sense of satisfaction was much stronger than Mary's desire to stop the lessons. Mother communicated this idea to Mary and let her make her own decision. Mary understood what her mother was saying to her. When the lessons become hard, Mary will recall her mother's words. She will remember that she is learning a skill that will someday give her great personal satisfaction.

Communication, then, is sending and receiving ideas and information. The skill is in sending the right kind of message in the right form.

SENDING

Human beings can send out all kinds of messages in many different forms such as these:

WRITE —

Dear Alice,

I have certainly missed you since your move to Chicago. All the gang here at Jefferson High School miss you...

SPEAK —

"Charlie, if you say that one more time, I am walking out of that door and down that street, and you're **never** going to see my face again. And another thing . . . ."

DRAW —

TOUCH —

GESTURE —

Terri stood at the edge of the playground, watching the other children playing. "Can I play, too?" she asked. One of the children waved her away with his hand. Terri understood the meaning of that wave only too well. She began to cry.

Thousands of messages are sent to us every day. By refusing to repair an old apartment building, the landlord sends a message that says, "I don't care about people." Building a new youth center is a city government's way of saying, "We care." What message do you think the poet Langston Hughes is sending in these lines from "Dream Variation"?

> Rest at pale evening . . .
> A tall slim tree . . .
> Night coming tenderly
> Black like me.

In a game such as charades (gesturing), the child sending the message must understand the knowledge and background of the other children if his communication is to be received successfully.

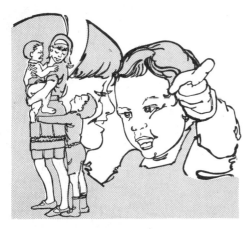

When a child sends a message by crying, gesturing, and trying to talk, do you receive the correct message?

RECEIVING

Sending a message is only one part of communicating. For complete communication to take place, the message must be received. Have you ever tried to understand what a child is trying to say to you? It is not easy to understand exactly what a child wants or needs. An experience like this shows, too, that children don't always understand what someone older is trying to communicate. Communicating with children requires patience and understanding.

Sometimes a child is not able to receive a message. Consider this example of Ray and his mother:

Mother: "Raymond, did you hear what I said? Close that window."

Ray: (Remains silent, staring into space.)

Mother: "Raymond, what is the matter with you?"

Ray: (No response.)

Mother: "What do I have to do to get your attention, Raymond? Should I send you a letter?"

That might not be a bad idea, Mother. Raymond is not receiving your message through his sense of hearing. He might be hard of hearing, or he might just be lost in his own thoughts. The main thing is that Raymond is not receiving the message. He has turned his mother off.

How can you communicate when someone has turned you off? Perhaps you have chosen the wrong form of communication.

Jack: "I really go for you, Lucy. You are a great person, a **real** person, you know? I hope you like me because I like you and if you like me and I like you, why when people like each other then that's pretty good, isn't it?"

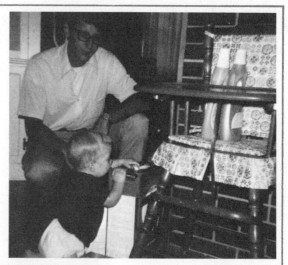

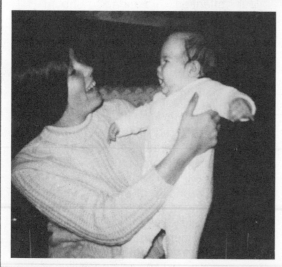

Children of all ages receive messages through their senses of seeing, hearing, tasting, smelling, and touching.

UNDERSTANDING - MISUNDERSTANDING

Lucy: "I don't understand you."

Jack: "Well, what I'm trying to say is —
I — I brought you these!" (He gives
Lucy five beautiful roses.)

Lucy: (smelling the flowers) "**Now** I
understand you."

Children can have a great difficulty in
understanding if the message is sent in the
wrong form. A tiny infant, for example, is
only capable of understanding sounds and
touches. As children grow, their ability to
receive more complex messages increases.

INFANCY
Mother holds her infant Susie and
hums a soft tune. The feeling of her
mother's body and the sound of her
voice makes Susie feel very secure —
just the message mother wanted to
send.

TWO YEARS
Susie has grown quite a bit. She can
now understand simple spoken language.

Mother: "Nighty night, Susie."
Susie: "Night, Mommy."

SIX YEARS
Just look at the change that has taken
place in four years. Susie is now able
to receive a variety of messages.

Mother: (holding picture book) "What's
the bear doing in this picture, Susie?"

Susie: "He's all sleepy and is going to
bed in his cave."

Mother: "Don't you think it's time for
you to go to bed, too?"

Susie: "All right, Mommy. I'll pretend
I'm a bear in a cave."

We can receive messages in other
ways, too. How would you receive the
following:

- A painting by Picasso?
- A song by the Rolling Stones?
- The fragrance of a flower?
- The taste of pie?
- A kind word or compliment from
someone you like very well?

UNDERSTANDING OR MISUNDERSTANDING

No matter how well you communicate,
your messages might sometimes be misunderstood. Consider the situations in the
art on page 39. You be the judge and decide
why these messages are understood or
misunderstood.

REVIEWING YOUR VOCABULARY

communication
conversation
exchange
language
satisfaction
denied
message
sending

forms
gesture
receiving
capable
complex
Picasso
misunderstood

INCREASING YOUR PERCEPTION

1. Explain the process of communication.
2. What methods of communication could
be used to send a message to an infant?
a toddler? a preschooler? an elementary
child?
3. What senses could an infant use to receive a message? a toddler? a preschooler? an elementary child?
4. What method of communication could
be used to send a message to an adult
by an infant? a toddler? a preschooler?
an elementary child?
5. Identify examples of communications between children and adults which you
have seen. Explain how the message
was sent and received.
6. Describe a communications misunderstanding that happened to you.

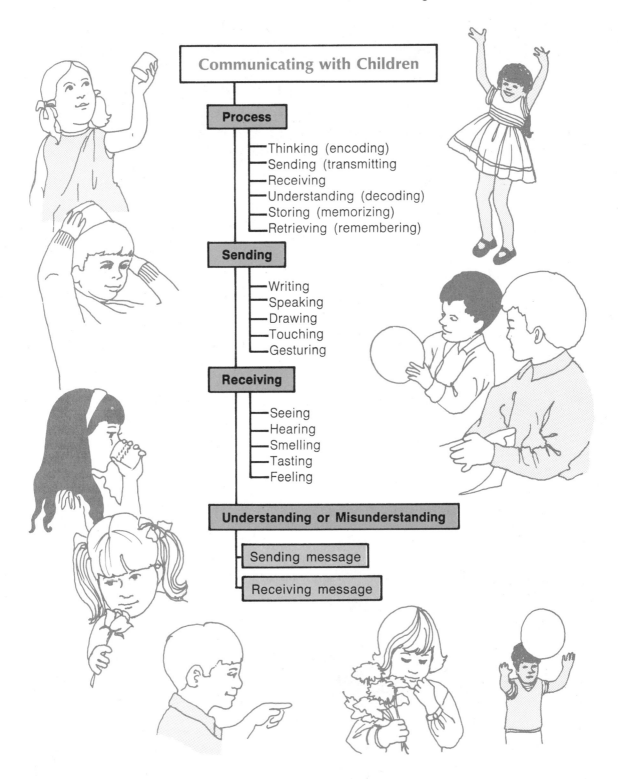

Communicating with Children

Process

— Thinking (encoding)
— Sending (transmitting
— Receiving
— Understanding (decoding)
— Storing (memorizing)
— Retrieving (remembering)

Sending

— Writing
— Speaking
— Drawing
— Touching
— Gesturing

Receiving

— Seeing
— Hearing
— Smelling
— Tasting
— Feeling

Understanding or Misunderstanding

Sending message

Receiving message

Reading 6

Story of the Kindergarten

Kathy Williams had been telling a story to her kindergarten class.

"Halloween," she said to the children, "is only a few weeks away. Does anyone know what children do on Halloween?"

"They dress up in funny clothes and get lots of candy to eat," said Billy.

"They act like witches and scare people," laughed Alice.

"I can scare you," cried Sandy. "BOO!"

All the children laughed. "Yes, we do some of these things on Halloween," said the kindergarten teacher. "We also have parties. Parties are a lot of fun. Would you like to have a Halloween party?"

The children became very excited. They all tried to talk at once, each shouting what he or she would do at the party. Kathy gently quieted them and then said, "If we're going to have a party, we have a lot to do. It's almost time to go home now, but tomorrow we will plan our party."

PLANNING

That night Kathy thought a great deal about the kind of party her kindergarten classes might have. She knew that successful parties, like other school activities, are carefully planned. The first thing Kathy had to consider in planning was money.

Kathy's school, like all public kindergartens, receives money from the government. The government receives its money through taxes paid by the public. A certain amount of money is set aside by the school board to pay school personnel for their work and to purchase books, toys, paper, paste, and other supplies. The school's principal also has a general fund (money) that can be used for special needs. Kathy could use some of that money to spend on her Halloween party. She wrote down the amount of money needed, knowing she could not spend more than that certain amount.

Kathy also thought about her classroom. The room was large and well lighted. There was enough space for the games and other children's activities for the party. There was plenty of storage space for them to store their Halloween costumes. Before eating their Halloween snacks, they could wash their hands at sinks that were set low enough for kindergarteners to use.

Teachers and principals are the school managers that plan, organize, and control the school curriculum, equipment, and instructional supplies.

By using the skills of a trained paraprofessional, the kindergarten teacher is able to manage learning activities that meet the needs of the students.

Good learning environments with well-planned buildings and equipment provide students with many learning experiences.

Kathy would need help with her party. Her **teacher aide**, a young woman who had recently graduated from high school, could help Kathy in decorating the room, keeping things in order, and even typing the party program. She could also use the help of a **paraprofessional**. This is a person with some college training who has been approved by the State Teacher Certification Board. The paraprofessional could read to the children and help Kathy lead them in games or songs. If Kathy decided to have a little snack for the children, workers in the school cafeteria would prepare it for her. During the party, the school's registered nurse would be available to mend a scraped knee or soothe an upset stomach. A friendly bus driver would bring the children to and from the kindergarten in safety. Kathy also

thought about asking some of the mothers of the children to help at the party.

The main problem for Kathy was the program. What kind of program would be best for the party? Each year the kindergarten staff planned the entire kindergarten program so that each child would be involved and each growing and learning need met. The program for the Halloween party should serve the same purpose. Kathy decided it might be both educational and fun for the children to help plan the program.

ORGANIZING

"We want some pumpkins."
"We want candy."
"We want to pin the tail on the turkey."
"It's not a turkey. It's a donkey."
Kathy clapped her hands once to bring the class back to order. "Let's talk about what we will need for our party. Would you like to make a jack-o'-lantern?"
The children said they would.

"Can we play pin the hat on the witch," asked Bobby?

"It's pin the tail on the donkey," said Juan.

"I think that games would be fun," replied Kathy.

"We need Halloween songs," said Alice.

"We need food," cried George, who liked to eat.

"Do we need anything else for our party?" asked Kathy.

The children thought that decorations, a game, food, and songs would make a nice party.

Kathy asked her aide to check the local stores for a pumpkin suitable for a jack-o'-lantern and to find supplies which the children could use for making other Halloween decorations. She asked her paraprofessional to go to the school library and find books about children's games and songs for Halloween. Kathy also asked the workers in the cafeteria to prepare light snacks for the children.

A well-organized teacher is able to provide kindergarteners with learning experiences that help prepare them for elementary school.

The kindergarten teacher then began to develop her program for the party. When her kindergarten program for the year was developed, she allowed for a great deal of personal freedom for the children. At the same time, the program included the teaching of knowledge and social rules.

In developing her Halloween party, Kathy would find a way to help children learn about Halloween while they enjoyed a party they had helped create.

Each day during the week before Halloween, the children made a new decoration. One day they made scary black witches. Another day they made ghosts from white construction paper. The day before the party the children and their teacher carved the pumpkin and were surprised when they counted over 100 seeds in the pumpkin. The children also selected the games they wanted to play and the songs they wanted to sing from the books brought in by the paraprofessional. They even decided on the type of snack they wanted.

Before the day of the party, Kathy carefully wrote out a program that organized each activity of the party into time slots.

10:00 to 10:15 a.m.
Singing of two Halloween songs.

10:15 to 10:30 a.m.
A discussion of the meaning of Halloween.

10:30 to 11:00 a.m.
Two games; pin the tail on the donkey and drop the handkerchief.

11:00 to 11:30 a.m.
Snack served.

11:30 to 11:45 a.m.
Paraprofessional will read a Halloween story.

CONTROLLING

The party was over. The children had all gone home. Kathy stood smiling in the middle of the empty, silent room. She felt pleased, for the party had been a great success.

"Kathy, may I come in?" Mr. Roland, the school principal, stood in the doorway.

"Yes, please do," said Kathy. "As you can see, we've just had a Halloween party."

"Did the children have a good time?" he asked.

"They had a wonderful time. I feel that they learned something, too."

"You seem to be enjoying your work, Kathy," said Mr. Roland. "You have been teaching now for just about two months. Is it all you had hoped it would be?"

"It's much more than I ever dreamed. You know, Mr. Roland, one thing I've learned is that a teacher must be a manager as well as instructor."

"That's very true. We're all managers, Kathy. You must manage this learning environment in the classroom, and you must plan your activities, organize your time and energy, and maintain control. I must do the same thing in my job."

"I think keeping control of my programs and children is one of the hardest things I must do," said Kathy. "For example, while directing each party activity today, I had to

continually check and make sure that each child was really involved. My teacher aide reported to me that one little girl was not having much fun. I discovered that she had a very sore throat, and I told the school nurse about it. If I hadn't been keeping control of things, I might never have found out about that illness."

"Yes, teaching in kindergarten keeps you on your toes. That's one reason I try to visit the teachers here as much as possible. I want to find out whether there are any problems that need correction. I guess I am a manager of managers."

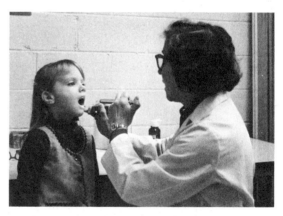

Management provides the services of a registered nurse to check and report illnesses and injuries.

The kindergarten teacher manages by planning, organizing, and controlling the learning activities of her students.

The teacher directs learning activities that encourage social and emotional responses from the children.

Kathy laughed. "I just never thought of myself as a manager when I began teaching."

"You must think of yourself as a manager if you are going to create meaningful learning experiences out of children's activities, rather than permit just a lot of noise and disorder. If I am to make this school an efficient and valuable place for both teachers and children, then I must also think of myself as a manager."

Kathy nodded. "Even the teacher learns in a school."

Mr. Roland laughed. "Yes, and even the principal learns, too."

REVIEWING YOUR VOCABULARY

kindergarten
planning
school board
school personnel
program
storage
teacher aide
paraprofessional

State Teacher
  Certification Board
staff
educational
organizing
personal freedom
social rules

activity
controlling
manager
instructor
learning
  environment
directing

INCREASING YOUR PERCEPTION

1. Identify people you know who are managers in families and enterprises.
2. List the processes performed by managers.
3. Give examples of how your family plans, organizes, and controls.
4. Identify ways you could plan, organize, and control your life.
5. Describe facilities that would be needed in a kindergarten to provide a good learning environment.
6. Identify the processes performed by the kindergarten managers, teachers, teacher aides, paraprofessionals, and custodians.
7. How can the knowledge gained from this reading about the kindergarten help you as a potential consumer of this service?

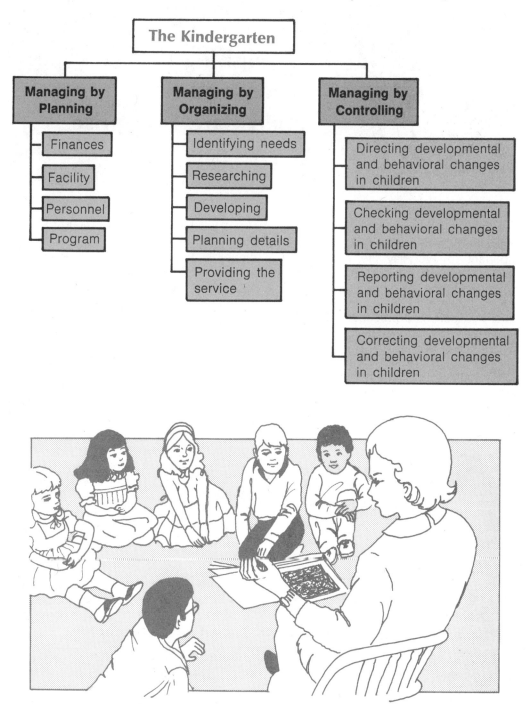

The Kindergarten

Managing by Planning
- Finances
- Facility
- Personnel
- Program

Managing by Organizing
- Identifying needs
- Researching
- Developing
- Planning details
- Providing the service

Managing by Controlling
- Directing developmental and behavioral changes in children
- Checking developmental and behavioral changes in children
- Reporting developmental and behavioral changes in children
- Correcting developmental and behavioral changes in children

Establishing the Family and the Child Care Enterprise

Have you ever wondered how families are established or enterprises begun? Both are important to everyday life, yet sometimes they are taken for granted. Families and enterprises seem to be near when they are needed. How do they get there? It is not by magic, but there is a process that works like magic in establishing families and enterprises. Using this process helps greatly in assuring the success of either venture. Perhaps a young couple named Pam and Ed can help you understand the establishing process.

Many couples marry to raise a family because they enjoy family relationships.

Pam Johnson and Ed Venturi had been dating for nearly a year. One night during dinner at the Johnson home, Pam and Ed announced their decision to get married. It was one of the biggest decisions they would ever make in their lives.

"We want our marriage to be a success," said Ed. "How do we get started in the right way, Mr. Johnson?"

Mr. Johnson smiled. "When a family is begun, certain things must be considered. You know, a family gets started much like an enterprise does. When I established my children's clothing store, I had a **purpose.** Providing clothing for children's protection was the way I wanted to earn my living. A family must have a purpose, too."

"We do have a purpose," said Pam. "We want to form a real partnership that will allow us both to grow as individuals. When we have children, we want to protect them as you have me. We want to give them a warm, loving home where they'll feel happy and secure. We want to make sure that they grow to be healthy adults and receive all the education they need and want."

Mrs. Johnson nodded. "I think you're off to a good start. Now, you should find out all you can about family life. Talking to an older couple like ourselves isn't a bad idea. You might also read books and articles on families or take a family living course in school."

Mr. Johnson agreed. "Yes, it's no different than getting a business started. I found out all I could before I went into busi-

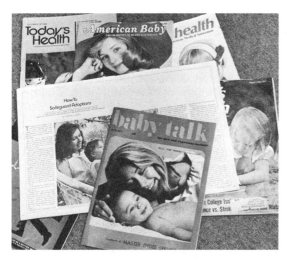

Families gather information from many sources, looking for ways to provide better care for their children.

ness. I knew that about 65 percent of the new enterprises fail during their first year of operation. I felt that the more I knew about children's clothing, the better chance I had of succeeding. Starting a family is much the same. The more you know about family living, the better the chance for a successful marriage."

Enterprises sometimes fail. Marriages sometimes fail, too. About **900,000 divorces** take place in the United States each year. Of that number, about 125,000 divorces are granted to couples married less than a year. That would mean that 5.5 percent of all marriages performed in a year would fall before 12 months had passed. An even sadder fact is that about 50 percent of teen-age marriages end in divorce.

"Well," said Ed. "One thing we know for sure is that we'll be equal partners in our marriage. When we buy a home, we will both own it. We'll also have equal ownership of our car and other belongings."

"That's an important decision," said Mr. Johnson. "I am the sole **owner** of my store. I could have chosen a **partnership** with someone, but I decided not to do so."

PROPRIETORSHIP

A. In a proprietorship, one person owns the enterprise.

PARTNERSHIP

B. In a partnership, two or more people own the enterprise.

CORPORATION

C. In a corporation, stockholders (people who buy shares in the enterprise) own the enterprise.

An enterprise must decide what type of ownership it will establish.

If his store had been a larger enterprise, Mr. Johnson might have formed a **corporation.** In a corporation, shares (stocks) are sold to other people. Each person who owns one or many shares would be one of the owners of the store. When the store made a profit, each owner would receive part of that profit called a **dividend.**

In a partnership, the responsibility of ownership is shared equally.

Who will prepare dinner and who will feed the baby are two policy decisions that can be determined by the family enterprise.

Pam smiled. "Ed and I do disagree about some things. He feels that we should only pay cash for the things we buy. That's a good idea, but we might have to borrow money to buy a house or car. Ed also believes in being rather strict with children. I guess I'm a little more permissive. I probably wouldn't spank them. Ed would."

Pam's mother laughed. "You'd better settle those differences as soon as you can. You'll need some guidelines in family life if you're to meet your goals."

"Many years ago," said Mr. Johnson, "I made a policy in my store to carry only a top quality of clothing. Just as in a family, enterprises must have certain rules to follow. Deciding the policies of my store took lots of time and thought. Both of you should spend some time deciding what rules you will have in your family."

Communicating will be one of the most important things for Pam and Ed to learn. Many marriages fail because husband and wife cannot communicate their ideas and make decisions they agree to use as their rules and policies. They must decide together how much money is to be spent, how many children to have, what kind of car to drive, and how to spend their leisure time. In an enterprise, decisions that will guide the business activities are also in the form of rules and policies.

"There are so many things to do," said Pam. "We both need to have blood tests at the doctor's office before we get married. We'll know then whether we are in good health. We need to find out what the waiting period is from the time we get our marriage license until we marry. Ed's going to the courthouse and will talk to the county clerk about this. We must also check with our insurance companies. We want to make sure that our policies are changed so that one of us receives the benefits from the life insurance if something should happen. There is so much to do, I don't know where to start."

"Yes," said Mr. Johnson. "I went through problems like that when I started business. My building had to meet fire and safety regulations. There were laws about the type of hospitalization program I could offer my employees. I had to register the name of my business in the county courthouse. I made sure, however, that all the necessary things were taken care of. Those laws are there to protect me as well as my employees and customers.''

When it is decided that a business will operate as a corporation, even more complex (complicated) laws must be observed. The enterprise must have a **charter.** This is a legal paper which a state issues, giving permission for the business to operate as a corporation. Usually, the enterprise seeks the help of a lawyer who will prepare the information needed to obtain the charter. The charter states (1) why the corporation is being formed, (2) what the corporation will be called, (3) who will operate it, (4) where the home office will be, and (5) what type and amount of stocks it will sell.

Bylaws are also written and explain the following:

1. The rules of the business.
2. Information about the selling of new stocks and the payment of dividends.

3. The kind of training the directors of the corporation should have.

For a marriage to begin, a license must be obtained from the state giving permission for a couple to marry. No further legal process is usually required for a marriage to take place.

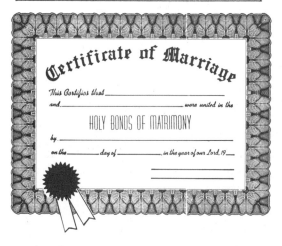

Legal permission must be received before a marriage or enterprise can begin to carry out its purpose.

Licensed day care centers are inspected periodically to qualify for child care services. This is one example of how the enterprise must meet laws and regulations.

"One subject we really must discuss is money," said Pam. "We must decide how much money we'll need to get married. We'll need to decide how much to spend on clothing, entertainment, and food. Buying a home is also a big expense. We may have to rent an apartment until we have saved enough money for a down payment on a home."

"I'm glad you are thinking about such things," said Mrs. Johnson. "Some couples just rush into marriage without ever finding out whether they have enough money for those expenses. Money problems can cause many marriages to fail. It is true in business, too."

"When Mr. Johnson started his business, he had to find out how much money he needed for paying **wages.** He also had to decide how much he would have to pay for the use of a building and for equipment, such as adding machines, cash registers, and utility services. The store had to be stocked with clothing. That also costs money. When he added all those costs, Mr. Johnson found that he would have to borrow money from a bank. Some of the money loaned to him paid for the building rent and equipment. Some of the money bought the clothing and paid the wages of employees.

"We'll need some furniture," said Ed. "We'll need to buy dishes and pots, pans, and linens. We'd better find out exactly what we need and how we plan to pay for it."

"Planning's the secret," said Mr. Johnson. "Always know **what** you'll need and **how** you'll pay for it. In my store, I set aside a certain amount of money for paying wages. I set aside other funds to buy new equipment and materials. My business would fail if I didn't do that. Can you imagine what would happen if I couldn't pay my em-

Decisions about how much money will be needed and how it will be spent must be made before an enterprise is established.

How well people and equipment are managed and cared for will help determine the success of an enterprise.

ployees for their work? When I buy new merchandise for the store, I've got to know just how many new dresses or jackets to purchase. I'd never stay in business if I ran out of children's clothes in the middle of the year and didn't have the money to buy more."

"Don't worry, Pam and Ed," said Mrs. Johnson. "Everything will work out all right. You are beginning family life in the best possible way. You are learning all you can about families, deciding what rules you will follow in a legal and personal sense, and finding out how much money you will spend on certain items."

"I think we'll be successful," replied Pam, confidently. "Beginning a family is a serious matter. It's one of the most important

actions we may ever take. It deserves thought and planning."

"I have faith in you both," said Mr. Johnson. "Now let's have some dessert! I'm still hungry."

Whether it is a family or an enterprise that is being established, the process is not simple, as you can see. Why, then, do so many marriages and enterprises fail during that first year of existence? Often time the reasons for failure can be found in the very beginnings of establishing the family or the enterprise. A successful venture in either case needs a well-planned beginning. This means having a purpose, making good decisions, abiding by the rules, and learning all you can to get off to a good start. Establishing a family or an enterprise is like building a house. How well it stands depends in large part on the foundation.

When a business enterprise fails, it often results in bankruptcy (being forced to stop operations). When a family enterprise fails, it often results in divorce.

REVIEWING YOUR VOCABULARY

established	regulations
operation	hospitalization
succeeding	employees
divorce	register
partnership	charter
corporation	bylaws
shares	directors
dividend	personnel wages
profit	stocked
permissive	legal
guidelines	existence
policy	

INCREASING YOUR PERCEPTION

1. Explain how the process of establishing a family and establishing an enterprise are alike.

2. Identify the purposes of a family and three local enterprises.
3. Discuss the type of ownership you would probably find in a family, an elementary school, a hospitality enterprise, or a toy factory.
4. Give examples of policy that might be used in a child care enterprise and in a family.
5. Explain the purpose of a marriage license and a corporation charter.
6. If you choose to establish a family or an enterprise, what are the steps you must follow?

Establishing the Family and the Child Care Enterprise

- Determining purpose

- Gathering information

- Deciding ownership

- Establishing policy

- Meeting laws and regulations

- Obtaining the charter or license

- Determining finance

- Identifying people and equipment

Understanding a Child's Educational Needs

Educating children is an important responsibility of adults. Too often, education is thought of as simply sending a child to school to learn the basic skills in reading, writing, and arithmetic. These skills are very important. True education, however, involves the family, community, and friends as well.

The most important part of educating children is to understand their needs. Therefore, parents and teachers must carefully analyze (study) children's learning needs. The entire process of education as well as the well-being of children depends on their meeting this responsibility.

EXAMINING CHILDREN'S EMOTIONAL NEEDS

Parents and teachers know that children need to learn about their emotions.

Playing basketball can help some children meet their need to learn physical coordination.

The ability to learn is different with each child.

Developing a good attitude about learning can help teach a child the value of education.

Education begins with the examination of children to determine their need to learn, ability to learn, and attitude toward learning.

Angers, fears, and sorrows are emotions that children must learn to understand and control. Those who cannot understand their fears may become tense and unsure. Children need to develop a sense of responsibility, independence, and self-confidence. It becomes important, then, that parents and teachers analyze children's behavior to determine whether there is a need for emotional education.

EXAMINING CHILDREN'S PHYSICAL NEEDS

Adults also analyze children's physical needs. Children must learn to control their bodies so they can walk, run, ride a bicycle, swim, and play games. When they have problems controlling their muscular movements, they may become embarrassed or afraid and may lack self-confidence. Children need the physical education that the

family, school, and community can provide. Physical education helps children enjoy themselves and have success when working and playing. Physical education also helps them maintain healthy bodies. They must be healthy before they can learn and before they can develop their knowledge or emotional behavior. Children need food, clothing, shelter, and exercise to maintain their physical health.

Schools provide organized activities to help children develop physical coordination.

Parents know that their children need to control their emotions and learn to be responsible for their actions.

By planning activities like bike riding, parents encourage their children to keep their bodies physically fit.

By helping mother measure the ingredients for a cake, this primary student is practicing the counting skills she will develop in school.

The first step in education is to examine the learning needs of children by testing their present knowledge.

EXAMINING CHILDREN'S MENTAL NEEDS

Adults analyze children's mental needs. Children need to learn about the world they live in. They must learn about their own needs, about nature, and about how people work and play. They need to learn skills that will help them to live and work with other people. They need to learn how to communicate knowledge, emotions, and thoughts to members of society. Children must learn much if they are to be happy and successful in this world. It is up to adults to **diagnose** (form an opinion of) **children's special needs for education.**

EXAMINING THOSE WHO TEACH CHILDREN

To help develop a child's knowledge and skills, education cannot be limited to the school and teachers. Education must begin and continue in the home. Who taught you to walk, to tie your shoes, or to control your behavior? Adults in your home probably helped you with these tasks. Education is everyone's job. No matter who educates children, there is a certain process that should be followed. The process begins in this way:

1. Examining the child to **determine** his or her level of development,
2. Gathering information about the learning needs, and
3. Diagnosing the child's learning needs.

After examining children and gathering information, adults diagnose the educational needs of children.

It is important to remember that children are **individuals** even though they can be classified by age, size, or abilities. Each is unique in his or her own way. Each child cannot learn in the same way as another can. A child may have special problems that must receive special attention. While Mary might learn to read at age five, Billy might learn only a few words at age 10. Although each child is different, each is equally important.

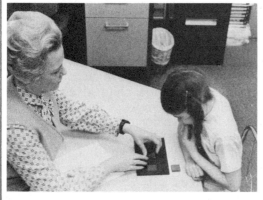

Some students are able to group new information quickly, while others are slower and may need special help and understanding.

Even though these girls are blind, they still have a good attitude about learning to cook in this special home economics class.

EXAMINING THE DEVELOPMENT LEVEL OF CHILDREN

Mother: "That is a rose."

Nancy: "I thought it was a flower."

Mother: "It is a flower. There are different kinds of flowers. This one is called a 'rose'."

Nancy: "I think it looks more like a flower."

Children have **different abilities to understand new knowledge.** Some children can understand new information quickly. Others are a little slower. Parents and teachers must examine closely each child's ability to understand. Children who are very quick or very slow to understand are **special children.** They are special because they will not fit into the average group.

Each day parents examine their children's ability to understand new knowledge or perform tasks as they are growing up. Most children have learned to walk at age two and a half. If the parents observe that a child has not shown any signs of learning to walk at that age, they are aware of a problem. They may have a **special child.**

Children have **different attitudes toward knowledge.**

Teacher: "The earth moves around the sun."

Andy: "Who cares?"

Andy has a poor attitude about learning. He may have trouble learning and his attitude shows it. He may have emotional problems. His teacher will examine this attitude closely, because the reason for this behavior must be identified if Andy is to be helped. Children with poor or negative (disagreeable) attitudes usually have learning problems and emotional needs that require understanding. Adults must learn to examine these children carefully and accurately.

Finally, children have **different abilities to use knowledge**. Betty may have been taught how to add and subtract, but, because of limited mental ability, she may not be able to use her knowledge. Adults must examine children's ability to use what they have been taught. If children find they can't use their knowledge, this will usually affect their attitude toward knowledge itself.

Father: "Now try to hit the baseball again, son."

Bobby: "I can't hit the ball. I've tried over and over. I don't want to learn this stupid game anyway."

RESEARCHING CHILDREN'S EDUCATIONAL ABILITIES

Adults have examined children's ability to understand new knowledge, their attitude toward learning, and their ability to use what they have learned. After a child's educational needs and abilities have been diagnosed or examined, the information is compared to facts already known about the learning abilities of all children. Is the child being examined an average child? Above average? Below average? Information must be gathered to determine the child's learning rate so that he or she can be given special assistance, if needed. Often researchers in education conduct studies to gather information about children's learning needs. The new knowledge they gain from these studies proves helpful to people and enterprises who provide products and services that meet children's educational needs.

Researchers have knowledge and experience that allows them to predict how one item of a study will fall into one of three ranges:

1. Below average
2. Average
3. Above average

Researchers know that they can test a large sample (group) of children (or a sample of any topic or item) and find these ranges. Suppose researchers want to find out about the developmental abilities of six-year-old children. Also, suppose there are approximately three million children in the United States who are six years old. The researchers could test the physical, mental, social, and emotional development of 1,000 of these children. The 1,000 children are a sample that represents all the children in the United States that are six years old. Researchers can use the results of these tests to find the abilities and growth characteristics of **an average child** at six years of age. Finding averages helps researchers classify the development of children.

To understand the concept of classification better, consider an example in which children's ability to understand various vocabulary words is to be measured. Assume that researchers select 1,000 words from the English language vocabulary and will test six-year-old children's knowledge of these words. For the test they will select 1,000 children at random (from any environment and with any kind of ability). The researchers will measure the children's abilities to understand the meaning of the selected words. The result of these tests will help them find the range for below average, average, and above average scores.

Suppose that researchers found that the group of 1,000 children scored as shown in the vocabulary research chart on page 61. This chart shows the test results of 1,000 six-year-old children's knowledge of 1,000 words. Read the labels above each column carefully. As you can see, 975 children (top,

3 MILLION CHILDREN 6 YEARS OLD SELECT 1000 FOR TEST AVERAGE

CHILD DEVELOPMENT RESEARCH

From the three-million population of six-year-olds, researchers will select 1,000 at random as a sample of the total population.

VOCABULARY RESEARCH FOR SIX-YEAR OLD CHILDREN

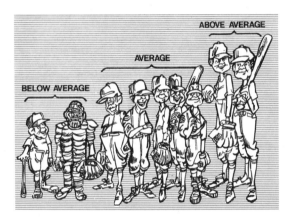

		Number of Words Understood by Children	Number of Children Age Six Reading the Words	Number of Children Age Six Who Did Not Understand Words
Below Average	−3 −2	0 - 150	975	25
		151 - 300	840	160
Average	−1 0	301 - 450	500	500
		451 - 600	160	840
Above Average	+1 +2	601 - 750	25	975
	+3	751 - 1000	0	1000

The average number of words understood by a child in this example is 300 to 600 words of the 1000 words presented.

Do you understand the words..
APPLE?
RUN?
STOP?

YES.
YES.
YES.

Researchers measure children's ability to understand the meaning of selected words by asking each child to identify the same words. The results of these tests are measured to find the average number of words identified by the children.

The height of each baseball player can place him into a category of average (about the same), above average (tall), or below average (short).

second column) understood 150 words of the 1,000 words presented to them. However, the column on the right shows that 25 children did not understand any of the 1,000 words.

According to the chart, researchers found that the average six-year-old child understood 300 to 600 words of the 1,000 presented. **Average** is the category with the largest number of children. A child that understood less than 300 words was classified as **below average.** A child that understood more than 600 words was classified as **above average.** Billy understood 350 words in the test. Would you classify Billy as below average, average, or above average? Mary understood 700 words. How would you classify her?

Researchers can establish the range of the children's ability to understand the selected words. From the vocabulary research chart, they can prepare a graph to illustrate better the abilities of children in categories of below average, average, and above average.

Study the graph on page 62. Find the line marked **−1.** Find the line marked

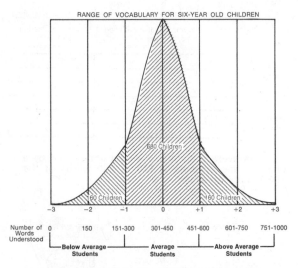

This graph shows the reading ability of 1,000 six-year old children who represent the 3,000,000 six-year-olds in the United States.

A reading specialist in the elementary school works with a child to overcome reading problems that would otherwise hinder her progress in class.

+1. The area above these two lines represents the 680 children who understood between 300 and 600 of the 1,000 words presented in the test. This is the average group of children.

What about the other children? By studying the graph, you can see that the remaining 320 children of the 1,000 tested are outside the average category. These 320 children are either above or below average. These are considered the **special children**. By their above average or below average scores, they have shown that they have special needs. Billy understood 350 words in the test. Where would you place Billy between the −1 and +1 lines of the graph? Mary understood 700 words. Near what line on the graph would you place her? What kind of program is needed for children that are in the below average group? Should it provide one of these:

1. A better family environment?
2. Individualized education?
3. Improved hearing, sight, or speech?

Now it is clear that there are special children on either side of average children. By using various other testing devices, re-

searchers can determine the abilities of children in all areas of physical, mental, social, and emotional development. In this way, they can identify the average child and the special child.

There are child care programs for special children. The purpose of these special programs, like the programs for average children, is to meet the needs and improve the abilities of special children where necessary. Some children have problems that handicap their abilities. A handicap can be any of the following:

1. Poor eyesight
2. Poor hearing
3. Loss of or inability to use a leg or arm
4. Poor reading ability
5. Inability to control emotions
6. Brain damage at birth or from injury

Child care workers help these children to improve their physical, mental, social, or emotional abilities so that they can make the very best of their abilities. Everyone is average in certain ways. Everyone is above and below average in other ways. The ways in which individuals are below average, average, and above average are what make them what they are — unique human beings unlike anyone else in the world.

EXAMINATION	RESEARCH	DIAGNOSIS

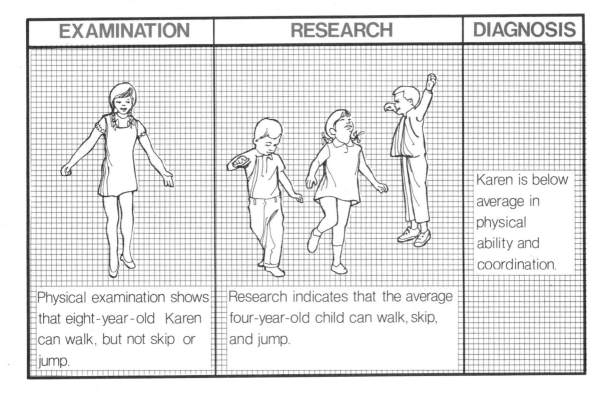

Karen is below average in physical ability and coordination.

Physical examination shows that eight-year-old Karen can walk, but not skip or jump.

Research indicates that the average four-year-old child can walk, skip, and jump.

DIAGNOSING

Information obtained from the examination and research of children is used by parents and educational specialists **to diagnose each child's learning needs.** Adults examine the abilities and attitudes of children as determined through research. They diagnose each child's educational needs by comparing this information to information which research provides about many children.

Most children have learning needs that can be met by parents at home or by teachers in nurseries, kindergartens, and elementary schools. Some children have very special needs that can only be met by educational specialists working in special programs. Whichever is the case, children's educational needs must be properly diagnosed so that their needs can be met.

Here are a few examples of the results of an educational examination and the related diagnosis:

1. **Examination:** Jane does not like to play ball with her sisters and brothers.
   Diagnosis: Jane is too young to hold or catch the ball. She cannot run as fast as the others. The ball hurts her when she tries to catch it.

2. **Examination:** Bobby does not want to go to school.
   Diagnosis: Bobby is having problems learning to read and the other students laugh at him. Bobby may have trouble hearing or seeing. Further examination is needed.

3. **Examination:** Mary and Billy will not play with the neighborhood children.

Diagnosis: Mary and Billy used to live in a neighborhood where the children teased and frightened them. They are both normal children and need to become confident that all children are not mean. The new neighborhood children are pleasant, and they like Mary and Billy.

REVIEWING YOUR VOCABULARY

analyze
diagnose
classified
special children
attitude
negative
accurately
ability

average
above average
below average
sample
concept of
  classification
random
individualized
handicap

INCREASING YOUR PERCEPTION

1. Explain the beginning steps in the process of education.

2. Develop a list that shows common educational needs for children at different age levels.

3. Give examples of different methods that can be used to examine (a) children's ability to understand new knowledge, (b) children's attitude toward knowledge, and (c) children's ability to use knowledge.

4. List sources of information you might gather to understand children's educational needs better.

5. Identify educational needs of children you know by examining, gathering information, and diagnosing the learning problem.

Understanding a Child's Educational Needs

Examining
- Ability to understand new knowledge
- Attitude toward knowledge
- Ability to use knowledge

Researching
- Gathering information
- Classifying information
- Testing
- Compiling

Diagnosing
- Emotional educational needs
- Physical educational needs
- Mental educational needs

Writing Educational Prescriptions for Children

Teacher: "We understand now why Kevin doesn't like school. He is very shy because he is rather awkward. He feels that the other children laugh at him. Because of that, he won't play games or take part in other group activities."

Parent: "Isn't there some way to help him? He's a very bright little boy. Learning should be an enjoyable experience for him."

The teacher must first understand the problem and then decide what kind of action should be taken to solve it.

Teacher: "Of course we can help him. We understand Kevin's problem. Now we must decide just what kind of action should be taken to solve his problem."

An important event is about to take place in six-year-old Kevin's life. His teacher is in the process of making a decision that can help change the way Kevin feels about himself. Just as a doctor writes a **prescription** (order) for a certain medicine that will cure a patient's illness, adults decide what actions should be taken to meet the educational needs of children.

Such decisions are made every day in homes and schools. Based on an understanding of children's educational needs, these decisions determine the following:

- Why education is needed.
- What kind of education is required.
- How education will be provided.
- When it should be provided.
- Where education should take place.
- Who the educator should be for each lesson in a child's life.

WHY WE EDUCATE

The first step in deciding what educational action should be prescribed is to determine why education is needed. There are two reasons. The first concerns children's **development**. Children start to develop as soon as life begins, and this development continues all through infancy, childhood, and adulthood. Throughout every stage of development, children need education. The songs the infant hears at bedtime may be the beginning of speech education. The parent's helping hands teach the toddler how to walk. The games parents and teachers play with preschoolers help educate their young bodies. Education is needed so that development can take place as it should.

Secondly, education is needed to help children learn proper **behavior**. The driver who knowingly speeds through a red light is endangering other people and showing lack of consideration of human life by such behavior. The person who cheats during a test did not **learn** how to behave during childhood. Education begins in the home when parents teach their children how to use a knife and fork properly, physically care for themselves, and share their toys with other children. In the more formal environment of school, children learn independence, responsibility, and how to gather and use knowledge.

WHAT EDUCATION IS NEEDED

"Kevin is awkward."

"Linda gets angry very easily."

"Sandra can't get along with other children."

"Jim is having problems in reading."

These are the kind of observations parents and teachers make as they discover what type of education is needed by children. These needs change as children grow. In kindergarten, for example, the following needs of children should be met:

- To develop muscles and coordination.
- To broaden their knowledge of the world and themselves.
- To have a balance of activity and rest.
- To be involved in both individual and group activities.

In elementary school, children's educational needs have broadened. Children

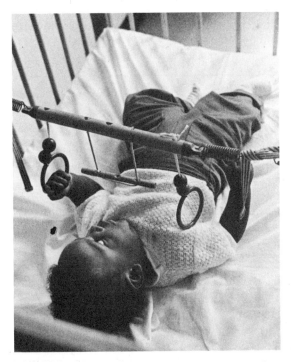

Playing with a toy can help this infant develop physical skills.

Behavior patterns are among the first lessons children learn at home.

must develop their abilities to work and play with others; become skillful in reasoning and logic; read, write, and speak their language; understand numbers; practice good safety habits; and have a basic understanding of science, government, and history. Special problems may require extra education.

The kindergarten program provides activities that help children develop their small muscles and coordination.

EDUCATIONAL PRESCRIPTION

Educational Problem: The child cannot communicate.

Prescription to Treat the Problem: The child should learn to read, write, talk, listen, touch, and recognize or identify different odors to communicate.

HOW TO MEET EDUCATIONAL NEEDS

When adults know why education is needed and what kind of education is needed, they must then decide **how** to meet those needs. This is usually done through a particular program that is designed for children of a certain age group. Parents often develop a program to toilet-train their children, teach them to walk, or develop their bodies.

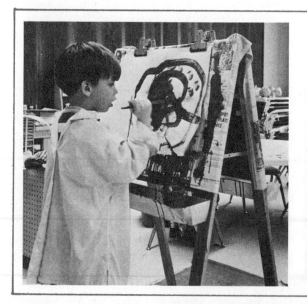

Children need to be involved in both individual and group activities.

The kindergarten has its own program that prepares children for elementary school. The program for one particular day may look like this:

8:30-8:45 a.m.	Sharing Time
8:45-9:30 a.m.	Work Period
9:30-10:00 a.m.	Free Play
10:00-10:20 a.m.	Music
10:20-10:40 a.m.	Snack
10:40-11:15 a.m.	Rest
11:15-11:45 a.m.	Storytelling

In the elementary school, the program must be designed to meet the needs of children ranging from five to 11 years of age. Elementary school children are in various stages of development, and for this reason the learning program differs for each grade and age group.

Programs for the **primary** grades (1 through 3) are designed to teach children to read and write. Arithmetic is often learned during other activities where numbers are used, such as in counting the number of children present in class. Science can be introduced by having children care for classroom animals like hamsters or fish; by gathering and classifying leaves, flowers, or insects; or by growing plants in the classroom. During the fourth, fifth, and sixth grades (often called the **intermediate** years of elementary school), children use their newly acquired skills in a program of lessons. These lessons may include social studies, science, language arts, physical education, and arithmetic.

Class periods in the intermediate grades are longer. Programs deal with separate subjects instead of general areas. The children are able to understand in more depth. In math such new concepts as division are introduced. The children also begin to acquire the basic rules of English grammar. In the **social studies** program, the children explore history, geography, sociology, and civics. They continue to develop their bodies through **physical education** and by receiving lessons in physical hygiene and good eating habits. Children may even be introduced to lessons in a foreign language.

Special programs have been created for children who have special educational needs. They are operated by schools, churches, state and federal governments, and different social organizations. In these programs children are helped either to **overcome** their handicaps or learn to **adjust** to

The planned program in this kindergarten includes work activities that are designed to give children physical, mental, and social-emotional learning experiences.

Basic skills in reading and writing are introduced to students in the primary grades.

them. The special program may be a part of a regular school program, take place in a day school for handicapped children, or be a part of total residential (institutional) care.

Some handicapped children are able to attend regular schools but, at the same time, may require special help. These children might be of normal intelligence. Their problem, however, may be in learning to read or in controlling their emotions. A specialist can meet with such a child several hours a week at the school or in the child's home. Regular schools have different kinds of specialists who can help handicapped children. One of them is the reading specialist, a teacher who has been trained to identify and treat reading problems. Another kind of specialist is the psychologist who understands emotional disturbances and can help the child overcome them.

For some special children, learning in the average school environment is nearly impossible. They must attend a special **day school** for handicapped children where programs have been designed to meet their special needs. Teachers who have been trained to instruct handicapped children are employed by these schools. During college, the teachers choose a particular area — such as deafness, mental retardation, or

blindness — in which to specialize. Teachers of the handicapped not only provide formal knowledge, but also help the children adjust to or overcome their disability.

Some handicapped children require total **residential care.** Their problems are severe enough that specialists must give them constant attention. Residential programs for handicapped children are designed to give them the total care they need. The children live in a special facility where their needs can be met day and night. Learning to eat or dress without help might be the limit of development for some children receiving residential care.

The residential care program requires many workers to care for the children who live in the facility. Specialists — such as teachers, nurses, psychologists and others — are employed to give the children special treatment and attention. Teachers help children learn to eat, to care physically for themselves, and often to learn a simple skill that will allow them to be a productive adult. Nurses and doctors may be needed to administer special medicine or treatment to children with serious handicaps. Psychologists work with children who have emotional or social problems. They help these children adjust to their handicap as best they can. Janitors provide sanitary facilities, and cooks prepare and serve meals to the children.

Some of these special children can be taught to read, write, and learn job skills. Both the day school and the residential care program help children individually and in a group. Both programs attempt to aid total development. A physically handicapped child, for example, receives exercise treatments from a physical therapist. However, the child also receives specialized help in mental, social, and emotional development.

The program for the blind child is not limited to simply teaching **braille.** Braille is the series of upraised dots that form the written language of blind people. The program must also teach the blind child how to dress, eat, and walk independently. Gen-

In the intermediate grades, longer class periods include more concentrated study of a wider variety of subjects.

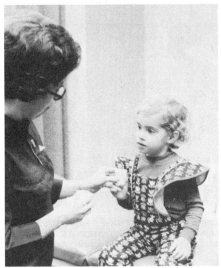

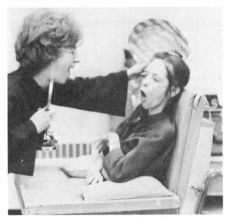

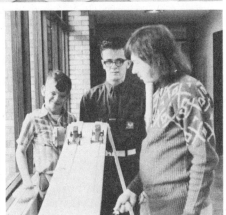

Some children have special physical, mental, or emotional needs that require educational programs which are carefully designed to meet those special needs.

eral education must take place too, so that someday the child can earn a living in the world of sighted people.

The mentally retarded (slow) child is involved in a program that helps him develop physically, mentally, socially, and emotionally as much as possible. There is a great range of abilities among the mentally retarded. Some children can only feed themselves. Others can learn to function almost as well as normal people. An important part of the program is designed to develop the child's self-respect and personal pride. Students learn to take pride in their grooming and dress. Retarded children must feel they have value as human beings.

EDUCATIONAL PRESCRIPTION

Educational Problem: How will the child learn to communicate?

Prescription to Treat the Problem: The child needs a program in which he or she is given personal attention while learning to communicate.

WHEN TO PROVIDE EDUCATION

At one month of age, Ann lies in her crib and watches the mobile turn above her. At nine months of age, she crawls and plays with her big, soft toys. At two years, Ann toddles about and is taken for trips in the park where she sees many new things. At age five, she can talk about the pictures she sees in books, eat her meals with a fork, share her toys with other children, and show better control of her desire to hit people when she is angry. By age seven, she is

By teaching mentally retarded people such basic knowledge and skills as bathing, dressing, or setting a table, they will learn to take care of their own needs.

Self-respect and personal pride in accomplishment of useful tasks are important goals for the handicapped child.

Children start learning and using communication skills at infancy and continue learning the rest of their lives.

learning to read, write, spell, and even stay all night at a friend's home.

The kind of education Ann receives at each age is designed for her mental, physical, and social maturity. Education is something that does not begin with kindergarten or first grade. Education is a process that begins during infancy when children learn to focus their eyes on colorful mobiles. It continues as toddlers learn to use their muscles in walking and as they grow into school age. When does education finally end? It should never end! People over 80 years old have learned to play musical instruments, drive automobiles, and even write books. Life is learning. Learning is life.

they learn the basic knowledge and skills necessary for high school and perhaps college.

Children with special educational problems often learn in special schools. Physically handicapped children, for example, may only begin learning how to use their bodies when they are three or four years old. Children with mental handicaps may live in a special facility where their needs can be met day and night.

EDUCATIONAL PRESCRIPTION

Educational Problem: When should the child learn to communicate?

Prescription to Treat the Problem: The child must be using and learning communication skills at infancy and continue learning the rest of his or her life.

EDUCATIONAL PRESCRIPTION

Educational Problem: Where should the child learn to communicate?

Prescription to Treat the Problem: The child should learn to communicate in the family, school, and community.

WHERE TO EDUCATE

A famous educator once said that the ideal school could be a log with a teacher sitting on one end and a student on the other. This means that education can take place anywhere. For most individuals, it begins in the home. Parents are the first teachers. Later, children may be sent to nursery schools to learn social and physical skills. Perhaps kindergarten will follow. Finally, children go to elementary school where

Education takes place everywhere — even on the playground.

WHO WILL EDUCATE

Just about everyone, including you, helps to educate children in some way. The child who sees you hold a door open for an elderly person learns this courtesy from you. Parents who show their children how to hold a glass, aid them in their first steps, and explain why the grass is green are teachers. Some people become specialists in providing education.

Everyone helps to educate children — even other children.

EDUCATIONAL PRESCRIPTION

Educational Problem. Who will educate the child to communicate?

Prescription to Treat the Problem: Parents, friends, other family members, teachers, and other community workers should help educate the child to communicate.

The **teacher** is an important person in the lives of children. Guided by the **principal** of the school, the teacher presents new knowledge to students, maintains discipline, plans learning programs, selects learning materials such as books, works individually with children, and discusses problems with concerned parents who are also educating their children at home.

Teachers are often assisted by teacher's aides who can grade papers, help with class projects, and perform other nonteaching tasks. Teachers may also receive help from a paraprofessional. Having some college training, the paraprofessional can as-

The school is managed by a principal who guides his staff of teachers, counselors, librarians, nurses, and many other workers through a program that meets planned educational prescriptions.

sume some of the teaching responsibilities under the direction of the teacher.

School counselors educate by helping children solve their problems. Counselors test and interview children, helping them to understand why they are having difficulties in certain areas. **School librarians** educate by maintaining an efficient library that will serve children's mental needs. The **school nurse** educates children in health care. For special children, there are teachers trained to provide education to the blind, deaf, emotionally disturbed, and the physically handicapped.

Deciding the kind of education children need is very important. Parents and educational specialists decide what a child's needs are and then **prescribe** educational treatment to meet those needs. By determining why education is needed, the kind of education necessary, how to meet children's educational needs, when and where to provide education, and who should educate, the parents and educators' decisions have the best chance of being the right ones.

REVIEWING YOUR VOCABULARY

educational needs	handicaps
prescription	residential care
development	psychologist
behavior	braille
primary	retarded children
intermediate	maturity
overcome	school counselor
adjust	physical therapist
day school	

INCREASING YOUR PERCEPTION

1. Explain the parts of a "prescription" for education.
2. List enterprises that provide education for children.
3. Identify workers who educate children.
4. Prepare an educational prescription for a child you know.

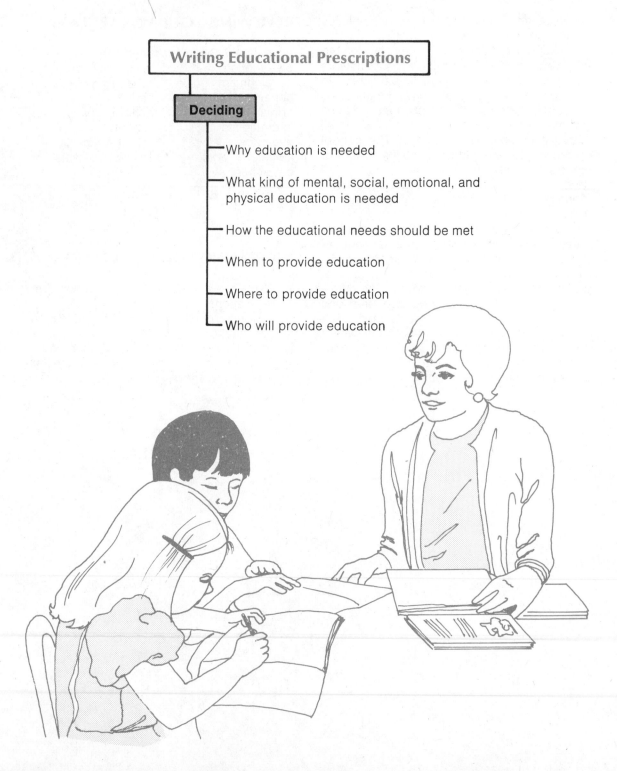

Writing Educational Prescriptions

Deciding

— Why education is needed

— What kind of mental, social, emotional, and physical education is needed

— How the educational needs should be met

— When to provide education

— Where to provide education

— Who will provide education

Selecting Resources and Methods to Teach Children

Teacher: "We understand Kevin's need to overcome his awkwardness. We also know that special help in physical education should correct Kevin's problem."

Parent: "What's the next step, then?"

Teacher: "We need to select the teaching methods and resources needed to make Kevin's physical education a success."

Resources and methods are the bridges which parents and the teachers use to reach children of all ages. Resources and methods provide ways to interest, encourage, teach, and help children so their needs can be met. The bridges must be carefully selected so that children will receive the education they need. It's as **simple** as that! It is as **serious** as that!

Most children really **want** to learn. As infants, toddlers, and preschoolers, they seek and enjoy every new piece of information that comes their way. Most children enter kindergarten or elementary school with that same interest in learning. What has happened then to such children as Janet, age 10?

Mother: "This report card is terrible. You are failing nearly every subject. You can do better work than this. What's wrong?"

Janet: "I hate school! I hate the teachers and all the dumb stuff I have to learn! I can't wait until I can quit and get a job and really have some fun."

The methods and resources used to teach Janet never reached her. If they don't reach Kevin, he also may wait for the day when he can **quit school.** Selecting the proper bridges by which children can be reached is an important part of education.

EXAMINING RESOURCES

Could you learn to read without **books** or **teachers**? Could you overcome a handicap by yourself if no one else had the **knowledge** to help you? How much fun would belonging to a school basketball team be if no **money** were available for uniforms or the services of a coach? Would you learn very much in school without **heat** or **electric lights**?

Children who are eager to learn and adults who are willing to teach are both important resources in education.

Resources are the foundations on which educational bridges are built. Before beginning any learning program for children, parents and teachers must make sure the necessary resources are there. For example, Kevin, who needs to overcome awkwardness, can be helped if the following conditions exist:

PEOPLE

If a physical education instructor is available.

KNOWLEDGE

If the instructor has the knowledge to do the job well.

FINANCE AND CAPITAL

If the school has the money with which to pay for the program.

INDUSTRIAL RESOURCES

If the necessary equipment for physical education is available.

UTILITY

If the community can supply heat, lighting, and other services.

Parents use resources to teach children, too. The little mobile that dances and twirls over a baby's head is an excellent resource in the development of eye muscles. The toys that parents give children are resources that are needed in mental and physical development. Did your parents read books about raising babies and children?

Did they keep your bedroom nice and warm during the winter? Think of all the many resources they used in helping provide for your educational needs!

EXAMINING METHODS OF TEACHING

You have been learning all of your life, but have you ever wondered **how** you were taught? Having examined their resources, your parents and teachers probably used one of three ways to project their knowledge to you: (1) showing, (2) telling, or (3) allowing you to discover.

Parent: "Watch me now. You button a shirt like this."

That is one way of teaching. Children can learn a great deal by watching others. Parents **show** their children how to walk, eat, dress, play games, and work. Children then try to learn these things themselves and, after practicing, are able to do them. Teachers often use this same method in school. "Here is the letter **A,**" the teacher may say while writing it on the black-

One method of teaching is to show children how to do something by doing it yourself.

board. For deaf children, being shown is a very important method of receiving knowledge. Teachers show them how to use the special sign language for the deaf. The deaf who learn to spell out words with their fingers can send and receive messages from those around them.

Children also learn by **listening.** They learn to talk by listening to the voices of others. Much of the knowledge children have is **told** to them by someone else. Small children can only listen to someone for short periods of time. Teachers in elementary school know this and are careful to provide other activities besides listening activities for very young children. As children grow older, they are able to listen for longer periods of time.

Blind children receive much of their knowledge by listening. Such common activities as eating are a simple matter for a sighted child. To a blind child, however, a plate of food is a confusing object. When a child has learned to tell time on a braille watch, a teacher can tell the child to think of the plate as a clock face. Chicken is at the 12 o'clock position, beans at the 3 o'clock position, and potatoes at the 6 o'clock posi-

tion. In this way the child can locate the food better on the plate.

All children (and adults, too) **discover** knowledge by asking **questions.** A toddler asks an endless stream of questions. During elementary school, teachers begin questioning the child. The teacher asks questions in such a way that the child is led step by step to discover the answer to a problem. Sometimes a parent or teacher may help children "discover" by letting them experiment. If a teacher allows children to experiment with red paint, blue paint, and yellow paint, they will discover that all the colors of the rainbow can be made by making different combinations of those three colors. Teaching children by allowing them to discover knowledge is one of the most challenging and rewarding methods of teaching.

The method of teaching that is selected depends upon the child's age and the educational need being met. Sometimes a combination of methods is used. For an awkward child, such as Kevin, **showing** him how to use his body would probably be most helpful. Another child might require a completely different approach in order for learning to take place.

Younger children pay more attention to lessons that involve showing and doing activities.

Providing materials with which children can experiment allows them to "discover" new knowledge.

DESIGNING THE LESSON

Available resources and the selected method of teaching are the foundations for the lesson. The lesson is the activity that carries the teacher's knowledge to the children. Every lesson used in homes and in schools must accomplish two purposes:

MAIN OBJECTIVES FOR DESIGNING THE LESSON:

1. ENCOURAGE CHILDREN TO WANT TO LEARN

2. INCREASE CHILDREN'S UNDERSTANDING OF SUBJECT BEING TAUGHT

This is not an easy task, and it requires much careful planning.

Parents design many lessons at home. Teaching children good health care, for example, is important. Children must learn to brush their teeth each day. Not doing so can lead to dental problems in adult life. Adulthood is so far away in children's minds, however, that such arguments as being "good for you" rarely make them want to brush their teeth. Therefore, the lesson must be designed in another way to motivate the child.

Father: "Karen, Mommy told me that you brushed your teeth all by yourself yesterday. I sure am proud of you. Big girls brush their teeth to keep them nice and healthy. I guess you are a big girl now."

Can you see how this praise might motivate a young child much more than being told to brush because it is good for her?

Lessons taught in kindergarten and elementary schools are designed as daily activities for children of many different ages. Teachers know that children in kindergarten or first grade cannot learn or understand in the same way as third or fifth grade students. Therefore, lessons for each grade level are designed differently to increase student learning. Study the objectives (goals) for daily lesson plans for children in grades one through six on page 81. The plans state what activities will be done at certain times of the day and what children should learn from each activity. Do you think these lessons will make children want to learn? Will they be able to understand the knowledge being presented?

In primary grades, children will be introduced to formal education and will learn basic skills in reading, writing, and math.

Objectives for Daily Lesson Plans

Time Schedule	Program	Today's Student Goal
FIRST GRADE		
8:30- 9:30 a.m.	Language Arts, Reading	to recognize the beginning sounds of some words starting with two consonants together: cl, br, ch
9:30-10:00 a.m.	Music	to clap a simple rhythm
10:00-10:30 a.m.	Physical Education	to develop muscle control in skipping and hopping
10:30-11:00 a.m.	Language Arts	to practice correctly forming f's in manuscript writing
11:00-11:25 a.m.	Social Studies	to understand the needs for rules and social order (citizenship) in the classroom
11:25-12:40 p.m.	Lunch	
12:40-1:20 p.m.	Math	to understand that numbers can be used to describe how many objects are in a group
1:20-2:10 p.m.	Recess and milk	
2:10-2:45 p.m.	Science	to observe and describe a frog
2:45-3:15 p.m.	Art	to experiment with finger paint
SECOND GRADE		
8:30-10:30 a.m.	Language Arts	to test memory and understanding of material read
10:30-10:45 a.m.	TV Art	to experiment with shapes
10:45-11:00 a.m.	Health and Physical Education	to understand and practice correct dental care
11:00-11:30 a.m.	Math	to practice subtraction with 9's
11:30-12:35 p.m.	Lunch	
12:35-1:20 p.m.	Library	to understand how to care for a book
1:20-1:30 p.m.	Oral Grammar	to compose a short friendly letter
1:30-1:45 p.m.	Recess	
1:45-2:15 p.m.	Story Time	to practice listening skills
2:15-2:40 p.m.	Science	to classify tree leaves
2:40-3:10 p.m.	Social Studies	to learn about families in Africa

Time Schedule	Program	Today's Student Goal
THIRD GRADE		
8:30-10:00 a.m.	Language Arts	to write a story about your most exciting adventure
10:00-10:10 a.m.	Recess	
10:10-10:50 a.m.	Math	to work story problems using units of measurement: pints and quarts
10:50-11:30 a.m.	Social Studies	to make a model of a pioneer cabin
11:30-12:30 p.m.	Lunch	
12:30-1:00 p.m.	Science	to investigate at what temperature water boils
1:00-1:30 p.m.	Language Arts	to discover what a contraction is: (do not — don't)
1:30-1:55 p.m.	Physical Education	to develop good sportsmanship in group games
1:55-2:45 p.m.	Language Arts	to read the stories "My Most Exciting Adventure" that were written this morning
2:45-3:20 p.m.	Music	to practice songs to be performed for the PTA
FOURTH GRADE		
8:30-9:15 a.m.	Physical Education	to develop physical coordination in softball
9:15-9:40 a.m.	Music	to become familiar with sounds, shape, and appearance of a trumpet
9:40-10:00 a.m.	Spelling	to test knowledge of 20 spelling words
10:00-10:40 a.m.	Art	to draw a picture of "Spring"
10:40-11:20 a.m.	Math	to work problems, using fractions
11:20-11:55 a.m.	Reading	to practice recognizing new words by using suffixes and prefixes
11:55-12:45 p.m.	Lunch	
12:45-1:00 p.m.	Story Time	to become familiar with children's good literature
1:00-2:00 p.m.	Language Arts	to practice silent reading
2:00-2:30 p.m.	Recess	
2:30-3:00 p.m.	Science	to investigate differences in rocks
3:00-3:30 p.m.	Social Studies	to discuss native customs and foods

FIFTH GRADE

8:50-9:15 a.m.	Music	to sing songs from around the world
9:15-10:00 a.m.	Reading	to develop awareness of different types of literature: poetry, stories, plays
10:00-10:30 a.m.	Recess	
10:30-10:50 a.m.	Language Arts	to use correct grammar in writing a story
10:50-11:30 a.m.	Art	to experiment with wire sculpture
11:30-11:55 a.m.	Math	to solve story problems
11:55-12:50 p.m.	Lunch	
12:50-2:25 p.m.	Science	to classify different kinds of insects
2:25-2:50 p.m.	Social Studies	to research the types of local employment
2:50-3:00 p.m.	Writing	to practice good penmanship in the writing workbook
3:00-3:40 p.m.	Physical Education	to learn the rules of soccer

SIXTH GRADE

8:40-9:00 a.m.	Math	to understand the differences and similarities between fractions and decimals
9:00-9:40 a.m.	Art	to understand how clay pots are made and fired
9:40-10:00 a.m.	Math	to practice converting fractions to decimals
10:00-10:20 a.m.	Library	to learn how to use the card catalog
10:20-10:45 a.m.	Recess	
10:45-11:05 a.m.	Math	to use decimals in solving story problems
11:05-11:30 a.m.	Music	to prepare to perform in the choir contest
11:30-11:55 a.m.	Spelling or Writing	to complete 25 exercises in the spelling workbook
11:55-12:55 p.m.	Lunch	
12:55-1:35 p.m.	Reading	to build reading speed
1:35-2:00 p.m.	Language Arts	to practice correct punctuation using colons and semicolons
2:00-2:25 p.m.	Social Studies	to plan a local ecology program
2:25-3:00 p.m.	Science	to conduct an experiment with algae and fungi to determine their benefits in an aquarium
3:00-3:30 p.m.	Physical Education (boys and girls in separate classes)	to develop a better understanding of puberty (reaching manhood and womanhood)

The elementary program begins in the primary grades. In the majority of schools, primary grades are grades one through three. The primary grades have these two purposes:

1. Introduce children to the process of formal education.
2. Provide children with basic skills in reading, writing, and math.

The primary grade teacher has an important responsibility. It is she who first presents the elementary school program to children in a self-contained classroom (one room where all of a child's classes are taught). It is she who must watch for any problems a child has that might hinder or prevent learning. Handicaps — such as poor eyesight, poor hearing, mental or emotional retardation — must be identified and treated as soon as possible. It is often the primary grade teacher who brings these matters to the attention of specialists who have the resources to deal with these problems.

The early identification of learning problems is greatly aided by the **I. Q. Test.** This test is usually given to students in the early primary grades. The initials "I. Q." stand for intelligence quotient. The test simply gives an estimate of a child's mental ability as compared to other children. A score of 90 to 110 is considered average. The test's main purpose is to help teachers identify students who need special help. Children may also take a **reading readiness test.** This test determines whether a student has the knowledge and experience needed to learn to read the materials at the same rate as other students in the class. If the text shows students are not ready for the textbooks planned for them, the teacher may select books to help them improve their abilities.

These tests are resources which aid the primary teacher in performing her most important job — that of presenting a program that will teach children to read and write. There are different ways to teach reading to young children with short attention spans. Three of them are (1) the phonic method, (2) analytical method, and (3) story method.

In the **phonic method,** children learn to use sounds while forming letters and

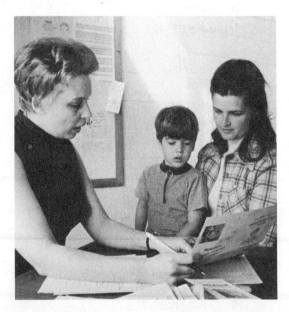

After children have been tested to find out their ability to learn, the teacher discusses the test results with parents.

A specialist teaches "signing" (forming words with hand movements) to a special student who is deaf.

words. In the **analytical method,** children first see how a particular word is used in a paragraph or sentence. Then they learn to recognize the word in other sentences. In the **story method,** the teacher may read her class a story in which a sentence is used again and again. The children retell the story. Next, they see the story in pictures and then in printed letters and words. Teachers often use a combination of these methods in their reading program. They must be willing to adjust their program to the abilities and needs of the students.

By the end of the third grade, children should be able to read fairly well and have a good reading vocabulary. **Remedial reading clinics** and classes that offer special help have been designed for children who have serious reading handicaps. Special teachers use models, charts, equipment, and an individualized program to help the students improve their reading ability.

During the primary grades, children acquire writing skills. Because their coordination and small muscles in their hands are not fully developed, children first learn to print in large block letters. They may begin by printing their names, other letters of the alphabet, and later a sentence. By the end of the third grade, the children are developing handwriting skills.

Arithmetic in many schools is often learned during other activities. Teachers let the students play games, such as "playing store," to help them understand numbers. Teachers may read stories that use numbers and let the children keep count of a name or animal mentioned. This teaching approach encourages the students to listen, concentrate, and learn to count.

Children also take part in other activities during the primary grades. They may be introduced to science through planting seeds, watching fish in a tank, and observing the changes in the seasons. They may sing songs, draw pictures, and learn about safety. The most important goal in primary grade programs is to provide the experiences and skills necessary for working with others,

continuing school, and learning about themselves.

By the end of third grade, the average student can read, write, do simple math, work well in a group, follow spoken directions, and express thoughts clearly. The student is also becoming increasingly independent. During the fourth, fifth, and sixth grades (often called the **intermediate years**

Learning activities are designed to provide students with the experiences and skills necessary for working with others.

During the later elementary years, students become increasingly independent in their studies.

of elementary school), students use their newly acquired skills in a program that includes social studies, science, language arts, physical education, and arithmetic.

Class periods, still held in the self-contained classroom, have increased from half an hour to about 40 minutes. More emphasis is placed on individual study and

A first-hand experience with live rabbits allows city children to discover what animals are really like.

Education becomes exciting and meaningful to children when the teacher has used the best possible resources and presented them in good programs and lessons.

exploration. Subjects are well defined as separate areas. The children have much longer attention spans in the intermediate grades. They are also achieving self-direction — a necessary ability for both education and adult life.

Teachers present programs of more depth and concentration than in the primary grades. In math, new concepts such as division are introduced. The skills of solving problems mentally, finding averages, and dealing with geometric concepts are presented. The students also begin to acquire some of the basic skills of English grammar. They learn how to use a dictionary, locate information in a library, and express themselves through creative writing.

Social studies also become an important subject. This involves a combination of history, geography, sociology, and civics. The students may do some work in science, discovering more about their natural environment and learning how living things adapt to that environment.

Physical education not only helps the children develop their growing bodies, but also teaches them how to care for their health. They learn basic food groups, physical hygiene, cleanliness, and good nutrition habits.

Intermediate children may be introduced to a foreign language. Children learn a foreign language much more quickly than most adults do. The excitement of a nine- or ten-year old learning French or German can be very rewarding to a language teacher.

By using all possible resources and selecting the correct method of teaching, adults present programs and lessons that will make learning exciting and meaningful. Think about the lessons you have received at home and in school. Did they make learning exciting? Did they help you to learn? If they failed, why? If they succeeded, what do you think was the reason? Parents and other adults have a difficult but exciting job as they create a learning environment for children.

REVIEWING YOUR VOCABULARY

resources
teaching methods
adult
puberty
self-contained
  classroom

I. Q. Test
intelligence quotient
reading readiness
  tests
phonic method

analytical method
story method
remedial reading
  clinic
geometric concepts

INCREASING YOUR PERCEPTION

1. What resources are needed to provide education to children?
2. Name and describe methods of teaching children.
3. Give examples of different ways you could help children learn by the discovery method.
4. Analyze classes you have attended today and identify the teaching method used by your teachers.
5. Why is the selection of proper methods and resources important in the teaching process?

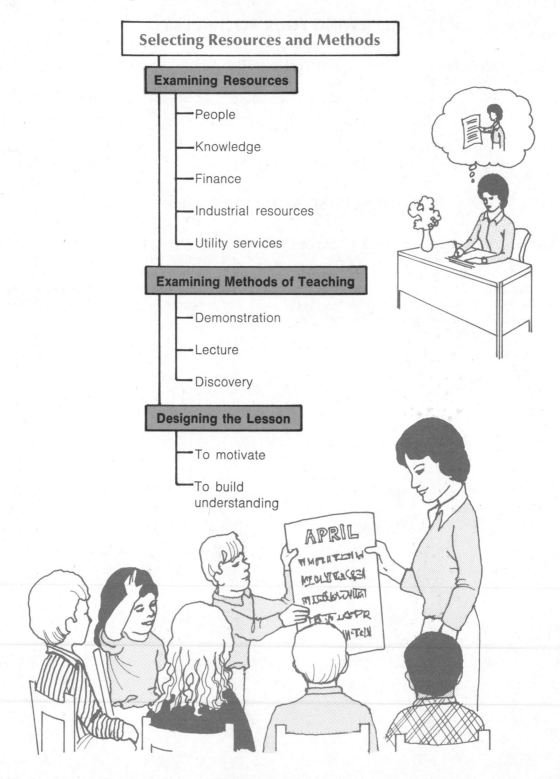

Selecting Resources and Methods

Examining Resources

- People
- Knowledge
- Finance
- Industrial resources
- Utility services

Examining Methods of Teaching

- Demonstration
- Lecture
- Discovery

Designing the Lesson

- To motivate
- To build understanding

Reading 11

Teaching and Educating Children

By teaching, adults educate children. Through their education, children learn the skills of walking, talking, reading, writing, controlling their emotions, and working with others. Providing education is one of the most important activities humans perform.

Teachers and parents are responsible for creating a learning environment. In this environment, children follow these steps in learning:

- They begin to **become aware** of knowledge and information.
- They begin to **imitate and repeat** knowledge and information.
- They begin to **practice** what they have learned.
- They begin to **perform** what they have learned.
- They become the **owners** of knowledge, information, and skills that make it possible for them to grow and develop into mature, responsible adults.

If children successfully complete each of these steps, true education can take place. Being educated does not mean that an individual has simply received knowledge and information. It means that a person is able to **use knowledge and information** in a way that changes his or her behavior. Education helps the crawling infant become the walking toddler. Education changes the kindergarten child who has not learned to read into the reading child in elementary school.

BECOMING AWARE

All education begins when an individual first **becomes aware of knowledge and information.** Through the senses of sight, hearing, touch, smell, and taste, infants become aware of the world around them. They become aware of hunger and learn that crying may bring food to satisfy their need.

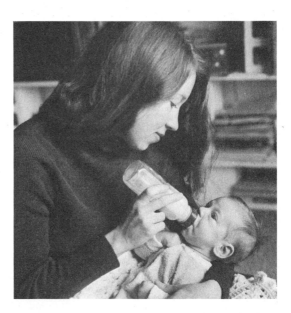

Infants use their senses of sight, hearing, touch, smell, and taste to become aware of their new world.

Adults help children become aware by telling and showing them new information.

Parents and teachers increase children's awareness by letting them experiment with color, texture, odors, and tastes.

Through the sense of touch, babies become aware of the warmth and comfort of being held close. When a toy is thrown out of reach, the infant becomes aware of the need to go to it and finally learns to crawl.

In a few years, infants grow to toddlers and on unsteady legs they begin to explore a bigger world. They discover new smells, sounds, tastes, and sights and begin to ask questions about these strange things. Why is the grass green? Who made the sky? Why are pickles sour and sugar sweet? Why does mommy or daddy work?

By nursery school age (three or four), children are aware of different shades of color and of rhythmic sounds in music. They have discovered the various odors of individual objects, such as paste and pies and the exciting tastes in food. They have discovered the different sensations in touching wood, wool, or brick.

Each new piece of knowledge or information expands the world of children and, in turn, creates new awareness. Through kindergarten and elementary school, children become increasingly aware of themselves as individuals and as members of social groups. They have long been aware of spoken language. Now they realize that, like adults, they must learn to read and write this language, understand math, and acquire knowledge about history, geography, and science. Their sense of sight introduces them to paintings, designs, and automobile engines. They hear different kinds of music. To understand these interesting things, they must learn.

Parents and teachers play an important part in increasing the child's awareness. By following a carefully prepared educational plan, adults make children aware of new sights, sounds, textures, and tastes. Adults make children aware of new knowledge by informing them, showing them, or guiding them toward discovery. Discovery, one of the real jobs of childhood, creates awareness. Awareness creates **a desire to learn**.

IMITATING

Have you ever seen a small child talk into a toy telephone? The child is imitating an adult skill. When children become aware of knowledge or information, they **imitate** and **repeat** it. After children become aware of speech, for example, they begin communicating by trying to imitate the speech of the adults around them. Infants are only

Children learn by imitating adults.

When children imitate, they are exploring and learning about things they see others do.

able to use sounds and gestures. Toddlers at 18 months of age, however, may say about 10 words. By age three, they understand about 1200 words. By age six, children can usually speak very well. It all begins with their imitating words heard day after day. Parents play an important role during this period, for they listen to their children's speech and gently correct mispronounced words. At one time in your life, you might have cried "wawa." Through your parents help, you learned to say "water."

Usually by age six, children have begun learning to read and write. Once again, imitating becomes an important step. A teacher may write the letter **A.** Children respond by printing the letter themselves.

As they learn, children often imitate everything they see. Not everything they see is good, and this may disturb them. Some children become emotionally handicapped

Each time children hang up their coats, they are applying and valuing their knowledge of classroom procedure.

because of something that troubles them. To help them, psychologists may give them dolls that can represent members of their families. As the children play with the dolls, they sometimes imitate troubling situations in the home. Observing their behavior helps the psychologist understand the child's problem better.

Psychologist: "Bobby, why is your daddy doll always so far away from the other dolls in the family?"

Bobby: "Because the daddy doll never comes home."

In this case, Bobby is imitating something that troubles him.

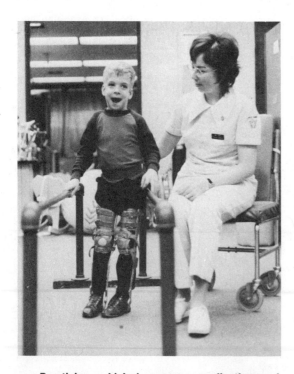

Practicing, which increases coordination and strengthens weak muscles, is an important step in training the handicapped child.

PRACTICING

You may have heard the expression, **practice makes perfect.** There is a great deal of truth in that. After children imitate, they begin to practice what they have learned. They do this by applying their knowledge or information and then deciding its value to them.

In nursery school or kindergarten, for example, children practice using their small muscles by cutting with scissors. They may spend a long time just cutting up paper or cloth in order to practice their new skill. The nursery school teacher allows the children to do as much for themselves as possible. Each child's progress is watched, and, when necessary, the teacher encourages the correct way to do things.

Jane: "One, two, three, six, five."

Teacher: "What are you doing, Jane?"

Jane: "Practicing counting."

Teacher: "That's very good. Let's practice the numbers in their correct order."

Each child in this music class is practicing individual musical skills as well as group social skills.

Sometimes children sit alone, talking to themselves. They are practicing speech. They may also practice speech by talking to adults. If an adult expresses difficulty in understanding the child's speech, the child realizes he or she must try harder to speak correctly.

As members of social groups, children are able to practice emotional and social skills. In the group, they must learn how to work and play with others and be responsible to the group as a whole. They practice consideration for others, loyalty, friendship, and sharing.

PERFORMING

Children move from practicing to performing what they have learned. At this stage, they are becoming truly skilled at using new knowledge or information. Performing is possible because the child has examined the knowledge or information, combined it with what he or she already knows, and has organized it into a form that will be useful.

In speech, for example, children first become aware of the need to talk if they are to make their needs known. They begin to imitate adult's speech. Nouns are usually learned first. "Water," the toddler shouts. Verbs come second. "Want water." Finally

adjectives are also used. "Big glass of water." Some practice is needed and for several years speech is polished and smoothed. In time, the child can perform the skill of using words in logical order. "I want a big glass of water, please."

Parents and teachers continually watch each child's performance — whether it be walking, talking, socializing, or reading — and correct mistakes where necessary.

Linda: "I didn't find no book about bugs."

Teacher: "I didn't find **any** book, Linda."

BECOMING OWNERS

The final part of the learning process is that of possessing or owning knowledge and information. This occurs when a fact or skill becomes a part of a child's total per-

Teachers prepare to "perform" their teaching skills even better by attending workshops or taking college courses.

"Performing" is using skills and knowledge in a way that is unique to the individual.

Through the learning process, children become the owners of self-confidence, responsibility, new skills, and knowledge.

Performing the best you can demonstrates that you "own" the skill and knowledge.

sonality. True education has then taken place.

At each stage of development, children become the owners of new knowledge. By the end of the nursery school program, children have learned how to work with others and be members of groups. They have learned new ways of expressing themselves through language, art, music, and play. Their behavior is more controlled, and they have discovered that they can do many things for themselves. Their bodies are stronger. They have developed some confidence in themselves.

The nursery school has contributed in many ways to the continuing development of children. What children gain in learning responsibility and acquiring self-confidence and new skills will help prepare them for the years of formal learning that lie ahead. All this is preparation for their roles as productive, independent adults who enjoy meaningful lives.

The kindergarten program has also contributed to the child's store of knowledge. During the school year, the teacher has constantly observes the preschooler's behavior. By keeping checklists, evaluation charts, and other forms, the teacher can tell whether each child is progressing satisfactorily. Does the child know how to keep clean, control emotions, try to understand others, and work in a group? Has the child's behavior reached that stage where he or she will be ready to enter first grade? Does the child have temper tantrums or show other undesirable behavior?

The kindergarten experience should also aid certain developmental changes in the child. The preschooler normally shows growth in these areas:

1. Curiosity
2. Responsibility as a group member
3. An understanding of self
4. An acceptance of self and other children
5. The ability to do things alone
6. Muscle coordination

At the end of the kindergarten year, the preschooler should feel more confident as an individual and as a member of a social group.

In elementary school, children become owners of even more knowledge. They have acquired a basic knowledge of themselves and the world around them. New experiences are broadening their outlook on society and providing a self-understanding very necessary to adulthood. Not only can they read, write, spell, and perform basic math, but they also have an understanding of history, science, geography, language, and art. At the end of elementary school, children depend less upon their parents and more upon themselves. They are owners of a sense of responsibility and of self-confidence.

In each stage of learning, children build their base of knowledge and information until at last they can perform the task or skill they have acquired. At this point, the knowledge becomes part of the child and permanently changes his or her behavior.

Sometimes, the educational process is not successful. A child may not learn a cer-

tain skill or may fail to acquire the knowledge needed to complete tasks or meet responsibilities as expected. Parents and

Teachers may ask questions to evaluate whether learning has taken place.

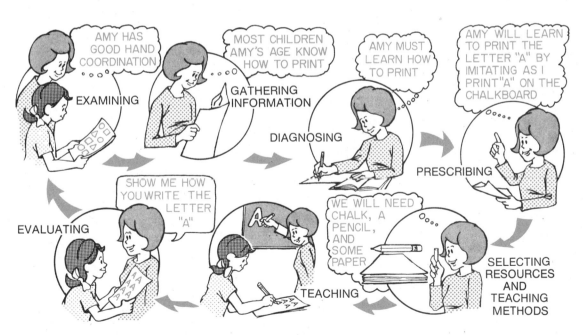

If evaluation shows that learning has not taken place, the cycle of education is repeated.

The process of education allows children the opportunity to experiment, discover, and learn about themselves and others.

teachers evaluate each step in the learning process by asking questions or observing the child's behavior. If evaluation tells the adult that the child is not learning, then the educational problem must be diagnosed again. This begins the entire cycle of education once more. Education is a never-ending process.

REVIEWING YOUR VOCABULARY

learning environment	social group	checklist
imitate	educational plan	evaluation chart
practice	mispronounced words	progressing
perform	consideration	tantrums
owner of knowledge	loyalty	curiosity
behavior	socializing	coordination
unsteady	self-confidence	evaluate
rhythmic sounds	productive	cycle
sensations		

INCREASING YOUR PERCEPTION

1. Identify the steps in learning new information and knowledge.

2. Create examples to show how children move from one stage of learning to the next.

3. Explain the importance of evaluation.
4. Diagram the entire educational process to show that the process of education is a never ending cycle, beginning with examining the child and ending with evaluating the child.

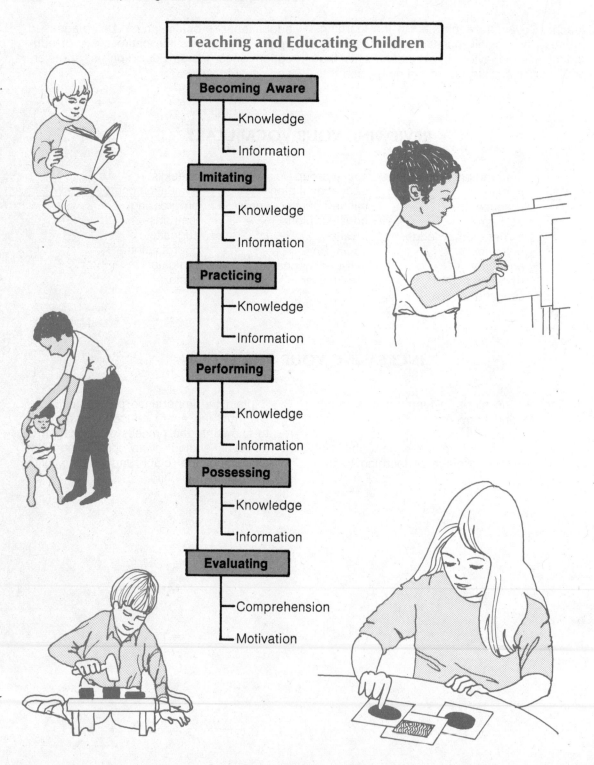

Teaching and Educating Children

Becoming Aware
—Knowledge
—Information

Imitating
—Knowledge
—Information

Practicing
—Knowledge
—Information

Performing
—Knowledge
—Information

Possessing
—Knowledge
—Information

Evaluating
—Comprehension
—Motivation

Reading 12

Understanding Protection Needs of Children

Children have very little defense against the big world around them. Their bodies, minds, and emotions can be easily harmed, and there is not much children can do about this. They must depend upon the adults in their society to protect them.

Many children are well protected. Their homes, schools, and play areas are clean and safe. They are given the proper food and opportunity for rest each day. Daily exercise develops their muscles and aids good health. The variety of sounds, sights, textures, aromas, and tastes in their environment encourages mental growth and stimulates their imagination.

Their emotional and social development is protected, too. Because concerned adults provide for such needs, protected children can form a positive and realistic self-concept early in life. They are encouraged to form good social habits and relationships so they can get along well with other people. In the following list are traits that describe individuals having positive social and emotional development. Examine them and ask yourself whether these traits describe you.

A secure home environment meets children's protective needs for food, shelter, clothing and exercise.

A protected child, with positive and realistic self-concepts, is able to explore and make friends with other children easily.

- Courteous
- Friendly
- Good-natured
- Considerate
- Sincere
- Fair

- Consistent
- Reliable
- Loyal
- Honest
- Productive
- Imaginative

If you have developed these traits, this shows some adults took an interest in you and your social and emotional growth. The environment that children live in and the people that influence them greatly affect a child's development. It is the adults who must provide protection. Fortunate children receive all the protection they need. Many children are not so fortunate. Notice in the following figures how many unfortunate children there were in the United States in one year.

The world is a hostile place in which to live to many delinquent, neglected, and dependent children.

141,000 cases of delinquent (behaving unlawfully) and neglected children were brought to courts.

240,000 children were living in foster homes.

75,700 children were living in institutions.

These are the battered, bruised, hungry, homeless, and angry children of society who found a not-very-kind world around them. The harm done them, whether intentionally or unintentionally, has now put them in the hands of adults who are concerned about their needs. These are children like 10-month-old Alice, who often cried in the night. Her tired, pregnant mother, disturbed by many personal problems, listened to the infant's cries for a long time. In one angry, unthinking moment, she poured boiling water on her child. Alice became one of about 65,000 children who are abused each year in the United States.

How can Alice and the thousands of other children find the protection they need so much? Often they are helped by child welfare agencies, such as the Department of Child and Family Services. Before help can be given, however, adults must reach an understanding of the protection needs of children by following these steps:

1. **Examining** the safety of an environment.

2. **Gathering information** about the child, the family, and the environment.

3. **Diagnosing** the child's needs for safety, protection, and comfort.

EXAMINING PROTECTION NEEDS

COUNTY POLICE INVESTIGATE POSSIBLE CHILD ABUSE

MAYFIELD — County authorities Friday were continuing their investigation into a case of possible child abuse.

A Mayfield girl, 3½, is being treated for injuries at Memorial Hospital. She was in "fairly good" condition Friday at the hospital.

County sheriff's police were called in to investigate by Dr. Joan Roberts, North Grove physician, after the little girl was taken to her office Thursday.

The tot, described as pretty and alert, was taken to the physician's office by her father when he became concerned about her condition, sheriff's police said. The injuries were inflicted early this week, according to police.

She is being treated for facial, arm, and leg injuries.

The child's right eye is blackened and swollen shut, her left eye is partially closed, and she incurred injuries to her thigh and arm, sheriff's police said. X-ray examination revealed that the child's skull was not fractured, according to the police.

Investigating officers have been told conflicting stories concerning how the injuries occurred, they said.

Temporary custody of the tot has been awarded to the Department of Child and Family Services, police said. Only the father is permitted to visit the child.

Filing of charges is pending completion of an investigation by sheriff's police, the state's attorney's office, and the Department of Child and Family Services.

Do you think this little girl was abused? After examining her at home, the father became concerned about his daughter's need for protection. The doctor's examination revealed that the injuries could have resulted from physical abuse. Police will examine (investigate) the case very carefully, for child abuse is a serious crime. They will question the little girl, her parents, relatives, and neighbors. During the investigation, the child will be protected by Child and Family Services. The agency will see that she is placed in a home where she will receive loving care until her case is decided. This agency exists to protect children from harm. By surveying and examining a child's condition, growth process, and the environment, adults can learn how well the child is being protected. The little girl in the newspaper story has not received the protective care children need.

GATHERING INFORMATION

In examining a child, adults can learn certain facts about his or her physical, mental, social and emotional needs for protection. Some children may cause adults concern because they are slow in learning how to get along with other children or are not developing mentally. Adults will begin then to gather information that will help them learn more about the child's problem and what may have brought it about. They may also gather information from reports and studies of researchers. As they study this information, adults become more understanding of a child's growth and development, environment, behavior, and the problem at hand.

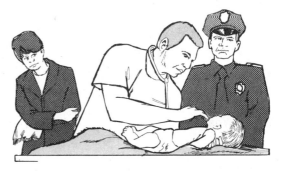

The doctor's examination may reveal injuries that could have resulted from physical abuse.

Child welfare agencies gather large amounts of information. They learn all they can about the major problems that exist in the community, the number of children who have these problems, where the children are, and the kinds of care they need.

This chart, for example, informs the Department of Child and Family Services of the number of child abuse reports in the state of Illinois between the years 1972 and 1973. Of the 1,160 cases reported in 1973, 53.9% involved boys. However, for the age group 14 through 15 years, twice as many girls were abused as boys. Notice also that the number of reports of child abuse rose from 1972 to 1973. This trend has been developing for some time, as the following chart shows.

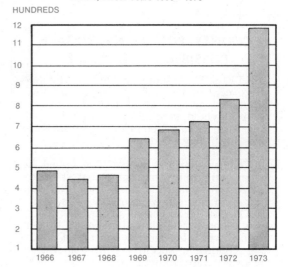

CHILD ABUSE REPORTS BY YEAR
Illinois, Fiscal Years 1966 - 1973

HUNDREDS

Number and Percent of Registered Child Abuse Reports
by Age, Group, and Sex, Illinois, Fiscal Years 1972 and 1973

Age and Group	Fiscal Year 1972						Fiscal Year 1973					
	Total		Male		Female		Total		Male		Female	
	No.	%	No.	%	No.	%	No.	%	No.	%	No.	%
Under 6 Months	120	14.4	71	15.1	49	13.4	164	14.1	92	14.7	72	13.4
6-11 Months	84	10.1	47	10.0	37	10.1	113	9.8	63	10.1	50	9.3
1-2 Years	268	32.1	154	32.8	114	31.2	355	30.6	206	33.0	149	27.9
3-5 Years	153	18.4	79	16.9	74	20.3	238	20.5	117	18.7	121	22.6
6-9 Years	102	12.2	58	12.4	44	12.1	152	13.1	80	12.8	72	13.5
10-13 Years	82	9.8	50	10.7	32	8.8	91	7.8	50	8.0	41	7.7
14-15 Years	25	3.0	10	2.1	15	4.1	47	4.1	17	2.7	30	5.6
TOTAL	834	100.0	469	100.0	365	100.0	1,160	100.0	625	100.0	535	100.0
				56.2		43.8		100.0		53.9		46.1

UNDERSTANDING A CHILD'S PROTECTION NEEDS

By gathering information, people in agencies — such as the Department of Child and Family Services — reach a better understanding of the protection needs of each child. **Social workers,** often called "case workers," give personal assistance to children. Assigned to a case, they are given the responsibility of helping a particular child. Social workers examine the situation involving the child and study all available information about the case.

Suppose a family has asked a child welfare agency to help them with the mental behavior problems of their child. A social worker may study the scores of the child's personality tests and analyze these scores to find out exactly where the child needs help. Results of mental tests which the child has taken may also be studied. These tests may tell the social worker about the child's ability to understand words, numbers, space and form relationships; to remember facts; and to reason or think. This information helps the social worker understand the child's need for mental protection.

Case aides help social workers gather information. They talk and listen to people, such as parents, friends, and neighbors of the child. They often go into homes to study a child's environment. Case aides organize the information obtained in interviews to help the social worker understand each case.

When parents become aware of a problem that interferes with their child's well-being, they gather all the information they can in order to provide protection for that child. Imagine for a moment that you are a parent and have noticed that your four-year-old child is not developing normal emotional behavior. The child is fearful, easily upset, and withdrawn. How would you gather information about your child's problem? You would probably talk to people, such as those listed below, who have close contact with the child.

Your spouse	Playmates
Grandparents	Neighbors
Babysitter	Family doctor

You would need to ask them such questions as: Have you noticed this behavior? What seems to bring on this behavior? Is this behavior related to the child's health? Is this behavior normal for a child this age?

DIAGNOSING

Using all the facts and knowledge learned during examining and gathering information, adults form a diagnosis (conclusion) about a child's protection needs.

Social workers may interview the child's family to gather information that will assist them in determining what help the child needs.

CHILD-BEATING MAY BE NO. 1 KILLER OF YOUNG

NEW YORK — The battered-child syndrome has "reached epidemic proportions" and may have become our No. 1 killer of the young, asserts a specialist in the problem.

Dr. Goodness, director of pediatrics at St. Vincent's Hospital in New York City, says "at least 700 children die each year at the hands of abusive parents." Dr. Goodness believes the mother is usually the guilty party. "More often than not the father just stands by passively, doing nothing," he says.

NEW HIGH IN STATE CHILD ABUSE CASES

SPRINGFIELD — A new high of child abuse cases reported to the Illinois Department of Children and Family Services in a month totaled 82 in February, Acting Director Mrs. Watchful said Friday.

Mrs. Watchful said the previous high for a month, since the state Child Abuse Law was passed in 1965, was 77 cases in April 1970. The average monthly number of reports is about 64, she added.

Mrs. Watchful said the new high may have been caused by more conscientious reporting by medical personnel.

Both of these newspaper articles report diagnoses formed by child protection workers. Both articles share the same diagnoses — that the child abuse is increasing at an alarming rate. One article states that more medical personnel, such as doctors and nurses, are reporting child abuse cases. In the other article a doctor is actually reporting cases to the public. The doctor has diagnosed that about 700 children die from abuse of parents and that the mother is normally the person most likely to abuse. In a report issued by the Illinois Department of Children and Family Services, the mother was also diagnosed as the most frequently suspected abuser.

Number and Percent of Suspected Abusers Reported
Illinois, Fiscal Years 1972 and 1973

Suspected Abuser	1972		1973	
	No.	%	No.	%
Father	155	18.6	210	18.1
Mother	286	34.3	395	34.1
Stepfather	60	7.2	81	7.0
Stepmother	9	1.1	16	1.4
Sibling	20	2.4	20	1.7
Relative	32	3.8	39	3.4
Babysitter	40	4.8	53	4.6
Neighbors	1	0.1	5	0.4
Foster Parents	3	0.4	6	0.5
Mother-Father	-	-	58	5.0
Mother-Stepfather	-	-	7	0.6
Paramour	-	-	52	4.5
Other	228	27.3	135	11.6
Unspecified	-	-	83	7.1
TOTAL	834	100.0	1,160	100.0

FINDING A REASON FOR ABUSE

Why are so many thousands of children beaten, abandoned, starved, and emotionally abused? Why have adults in charge of these children neglected their responsibilities in such damaging ways? A psychiatrist (physician who specializes in mental illness) has reached a diagnosis of these adults.

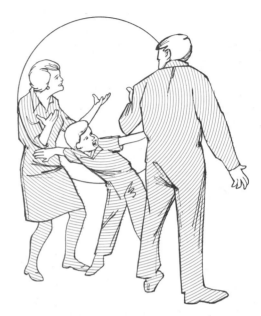

Parents who raise their children in an environment of constant conflict and unpleasantness may be behaving in the same manner they, as children, saw their parents behave.

STRESS
Abusive Parents Just Repeating Childhood Patterns — Psychiatrist

CHICAGO — A Denver psychiatry professor says he thinks parents who abuse children do so because they are trying to be good parents and because they themselves were abused as children.

These parents treat the child as a "miniature adult," the psychiatrist, Dr. Brandt Steel of the University of Colorado and the Denver Psychoanalytic Institute, said Thursday night.

The Denver area has had a pioneering program in recognizing abusive parents and helping them.

Steel told a news conference that although the incidence of child abuse is decreasing, there are 60,000 to 70,000 cases a year in the United States.

"Abusive parents, almost without exception, were themselves abused children," Steel said.

"They repeat with their own children the pattern of child rearing they experienced with their parents," he added.

"With or without serious physical abuse, they were raised in the same atmosphere of demand, disregard, criticism, and punishment," he said.

The psychiatrist said that as adults they show the same emotional problems that are seen in abused and neglected children.

Examining, gathering information, and diagnosing are the activities that enable adults to achieve an understanding of the protection needs of children. If the child's protection needs are being met, adults have been successful. If adults understand that a child is not being protected, adult responsibility demands that some action be taken. The neglected and abused children of today will become the adults of tomorrow. What kind of adults will they be unless they receive the protection they need?

REVIEWING YOUR VOCABULARY

traits	delinquent
defense	neglected
protection	foster home
positive	institution
realistic	abused
courteous	Children and Family
considerate	Services
consistent	case aids
reliable	spouse
productive	diagnosis
environment	suspected
fortunate	abuser

INCREASING YOUR PERCEPTION

1. Identify the protection needs of children.
2. Explain how parents gather information about children's protection needs.
3. Explain how protection workers gather information about children's protection needs.
4. Identify the characteristics of a child developing normally.
5. Describe the characteristics of an environment in which a child can grow and develop normally.
6. Describe an environment that would hinder a child's normal growth and development.

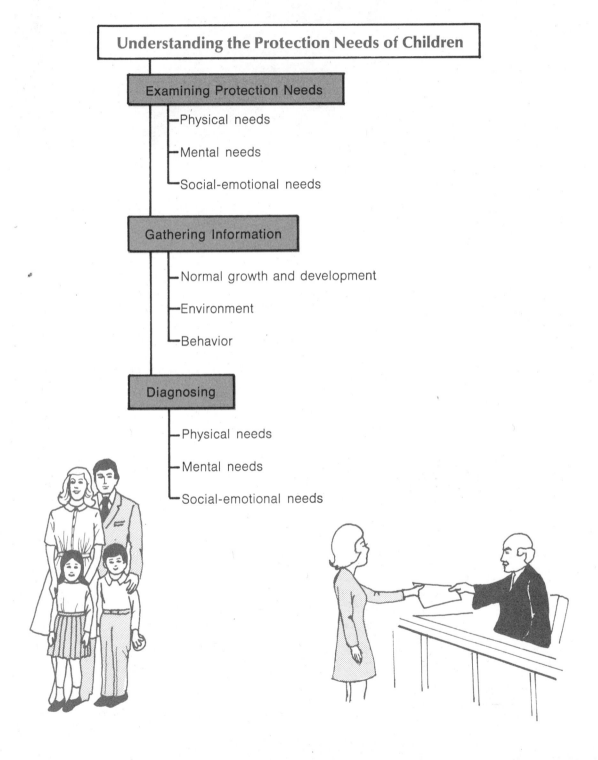

Understanding the Protection Needs of Children

Examining Protection Needs
- Physical needs
- Mental needs
- Social-emotional needs

Gathering Information
- Normal growth and development
- Environment
- Behavior

Diagnosing
- Physical needs
- Mental needs
- Social-emotional needs

Planning to Protect Children

The teen-age boy slumped in the chair. Nearby, the police dispatcher's radio crackled with communications from police in different parts of the city. The young boy had been the subject of one of these messages just a short time ago because police had discovered him breaking into a grocery store. He was now in police headquarters — a badly frightened and lonely person.

An important part of law enforcement is protecting the rights of people — the rights of the offender as well as the offended.

A police officer sat down next to the boy and began reading this message:

Miranda Warning

1. You have the right to remain silent.
2. Anything you say can and will be used against you in a court of law.
3. You have the right to talk to a lawyer and have him present with you while you are being questioned.
4. If you cannot afford to hire a lawyer, one will be appointed to represent you before any questioning, if you wish.
5. You can decide at any time to exercise these rights and not answer any questions or make any statements.

Waiver

After the warning and in order to secure a waiver, the following questions should be asked and an affirmative reply secured to each question.
1. Do you understand each of these rights I have explained to you?
2. Having these rights in mind, do you wish to talk to us now?

Because not everyone is aware of the right to protection, society demands that law enforcement officers read this warning to those who break the law.

The message protects the rights of the young man. It is part of a **plan** to inform people of their right to protect themselves when being questioned by police. The teenage boy did not seem to understand, however. He just stared at the police officer. Suddenly realizing what was wrong, the officer then read the same message in Spanish.

Miranda Warning

1. Ud. tiene el derecho de quedarse callado. empleara en contra de Ud. en eljuzgado.
2. Cualquier cosa que diga puede emplearse y se.
3. Ud. tiene el derecho de hablar con un abogado y de pedirle que este presente mientras lo interrogan a Ud.
4. Si Ud. no puede pagar a un abogado, se nombrara uno para representario antes de que lo interroguen, si lo desea Ud.
5. Ud. puede decidir cuando quiera ejercer estos derechos y no contestar ningunas preguntas ni hacer ningunas declaraciones.

Waiver

After the warning and in order to secure a waiver, the following questions should be asked and an affirmative reply secured to each question.
1. ¿ Entiende Ud. cada uno de estos derechos que le he explicado?
2. Teniendo en cuenta estos derechos, quiere Ud. hablar con nosotros ahora?

Now the boy understood his rights. Because many Spanish-speaking people live in this city, the courts of law have **planned** for their legal protection by having the message printed in Spanish as well as English.

Adults are responsible for planning protection for the troubled and troubling children in their community. Through planning, adults can develop the services that will provide protection in the best possible way. The first step is to determine protection needs.

DETERMINING PROTECTION NEEDS

Protection needs of children are determined through examining, gathering information, and diagnosing. The staff of social workers in adoption agencies, for example, examine, gather information, and identify the needs of each child being protected by the agency. Aides help the social workers prepare case studies by researching the background of children and adopting parents. These aides gather, compile, sort, and classify information that will assist the social worker in diagnosing human needs. Psychologists analyze each child waiting for adoption. They can give the social worker a better understanding of a child's social and emotional stability and mental ability. Physicians, lawyers, and clergy also aid the social worker in gathering information about the child's protective needs.

Pictures of homeless children are familiar sights, but have you ever wondered who is responsible for their care and protection?

As you can see in the following chart, the number of adoptions of homeless children in the United States has been increasing for a number of years.

U.S. ADOPTIONS

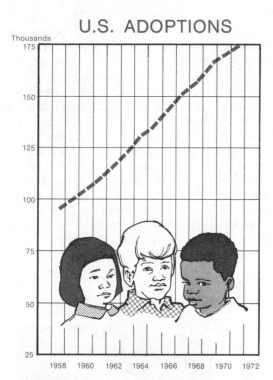

The actual number of youngsters available for adoption has **decreased** while the number of adults wishing to adopt children has **increased.** This situation has led to a large number of **illegal** adoptions in which couples must pay money to obtain a child. In adoptions such as this, children are sold with false birth certificates. Adoptions are sometimes arranged by interested individuals, such as doctors or clergy, who are **not licensed** to perform this service. Both forms of adoption seriously threaten the protective needs of children. These children may be placed in homes not suited for them or may be reclaimed by the natural mother or father. Great emotional harm can be done to a small child suddenly taken from a family that had not followed adoption laws.

The younger children are, the less they are aware of dangers, and the more they need the protection of adults.

Protection programs are designed to protect children from such dangers. About $550 million is spent for these and other child welfare services in the United States. That is a large investment. Large or small, don't you think the money is worth the future of every single child?

DESIGNING A PROTECTION PROGRAM

Protection programs offer four kinds of protection:
1. Physical safety
2. Legal safety
3. Mental safety
4. Social-emotional safety

PHYSICAL SAFETY PROGRAMS

Many physical safety programs are designed by parents at home, because the backyard, the neighborhood, and the busy streets can be dangerous places for their children. Parents may design a program, for example, to protect their children from strangers. Not all strangers who appear in children's environments are dangerous, but some might be. The parents can request a small booklet from the police that explains how children can protect themselves. Parents and their children can read the booklet. Do you think the message shown here helps promote children's physical safety needs?

REMEMBER KIDS, THAT FRIENDLY STRANGER COULD TURN OUT TO BE A TERRIBLE DANGER.

HE MAY SEEM LIKE A FRIEND,
AND KNOW YOUR NAME,
BUT IF YOUR FOLKS DON'T KNOW HIM,
HE IS A STRANGER JUST THE SAME.

A REST ROOM IS ONE PLACE
YOU SHOULD NEVER PLAY NEAR
BECAUSE DANGEROUS STRANGERS
ARE SOMETIMES FOUND HERE.

NEVER GO FOR A RIDE
IN AN AUTOMOBILE
WHEN THERE IS A STRANGER
BEHIND THE WHEEL.

Helping children meet their need for physical safety in crossing streets is the concern of both parents and police.

By observing bicycle safety rules and traffic laws, a child meets some of his or her own protection needs.

Many children are hurt or killed on busy streets. Parents show their children how to cross streets by obeying traffic signals or by judging the distance of approaching automobiles should there be no signals. Children on bicycles can present special physical safety problems. In many communities, police have designed programs that promote bicycle safety. Presented in the schools by police, the programs are designed to teach children knowledge of the bicycle, rules of safety, and bicycle care. Do you think that children's lives are saved by such programs?

Rules of Bicycle Safety

1. Obey all traffic laws, signs and signals.
2. Keep to the right and close to the curb or side of the road.
3. Keep brakes, lights, reflectors, horn or bell, and other safety devices in good working condition.
4. Learn and use the hand signals for turns and stops.
5. Give pedestrians and vehicles the right of way.
6. Avoid riding after dark, then only if the bicycle has a headlight and red taillight or reflector. Wear something white.
7. Do not speed, race or weave in and out of traffic.
8. Do not carry passengers or big packages.
9. Never hitch on to a truck, car or moving vehicle.
10. Travel in single file when riding with others.
11. Keep both hands on the handle bars, except to signal a stop or turn.
12. Slow down at intersections.
13. Dismount and walk across dangerous intersections or streets. Do not turn or cross unless it is safe.
14. Never squeeze into narrow places or between two automobiles.
15. Avoid busy streets or highways. Bicycles are not allowed on most Expressways, Toll Roads or Interstates.
16. Never ride out of a blind alley on to the street or highway without stopping.

LEGAL SAFETY PROGRAMS

Legal safety programs are designed by local, state, and federal governments; police; and courts. At the beginning of this reading, a teen-age boy was told his legal rights by police. A law, commonly called the "Miranda Warning," demands that people must be told their rights for their own protection. This law is based on a decision handed down by the Supreme Court of the United States. The Court stated that police must inform a person of his or her right to remain silent and to have a lawyer present before being questioned. The name **Miranda** is taken from the case (Miranda **v.** Arizona) from which the Supreme Court made its ruling.

Adoption agencies design programs that bring legal safety to both the homeless children and the adopting parents. The adoption agency program is designed around these activities:

- **INTERVIEWING**
Information is obtained about the physical, mental, social, and emotional characteristics of children who are to be adopted and parents who wish to adopt.

- **LISTING**
This information is organized and compiled in a special listing book used by the agency to find parents for adoptive children.

- **RESEARCHING**

Prospective parents are visited in their homes. Their personal references, financial situation, and ability to provide love, affection, and security are studied. Social workers or case aides gather this information and complie it in a case study report.

- **PLACING**
A child is temporarily placed with prospective parents in the home. The agency continues to have legal responsibility for the child until the courts grant the parents permission to adopt the child as their own.

- **ADOPTING**
Legal responsibility for the child is transferred from the agency to the parents.

Abused children also require legal safety. At one time, child abuse was a "silent crime." In other words, few cases of suspected child abuse were reported to police or departments of children and family services. Programs were needed that would improve the legal safety of abused children. After careful study of the problem, **bills** (suggested laws) were introduced into state legislatures, requiring all doctors and hospitals to report suspected cases of child abuse. In some states, police would then have the authority to remove abused children from their homes for a period of 36 hours. The court would then take further action.

MENTAL SAFETY PROGRAMS

Mental safety programs are designed to educate parents and children. Mental health centers in counties may offer programs that aid troubled families.

Four-year-old Bobby was a dull, withdrawn child. He had very little interest in the world around him. His parents became concerned and took Bobby to their county mental health center. After interviewing the family, the staff at the center suggested that Bobby and his parents take part in a family counseling program. This program was designed to help each family member understand his or her relationship with

Understanding their relationship to one another can help a parent and child maintain good mental health.

the other members. Each week they talked with a psychologist for several hours until they were able to understand and solve their problems.

SOCIAL AND EMOTIONAL SAFETY PROGRAMS

Social and emotional safety programs are especially important for homeless children. The love and warmth of family relationships are denied them. An individual can suffer life-long social and emotional damage as a result of a childhood spent in an indifferent, lonely, or even frightening environment. Child welfare agencies have designed programs that temporarily place homeless children with foster parents. Foster parents are families who are willing to share their home and affection with a homeless child until a permanent home can be found. Work-

ing closely with the social worker, the foster parents meet the needs of the child for a family atmosphere and personal concern and attention. Their protection often helps homeless children learn again how to love, laugh, play, and form relationships with other human beings.

Planning to protect children involves two activities: (1) determining the protection needs of children and (2) designing programs that will meet those needs. Think about your school and community for a moment. What type of protection programs have been designed? Do you think the programs are valuable? What changes would you make in these programs?

REVIEWING YOUR VOCABULARY

dispatcher
legal
illegal
compile
classify
diagnose
psychologists
birth certificates
reclaimed

Miranda Case
interviewing
listing
placing
adoption
bills
legislative
authority

INCREASING YOUR PERCEPTION

1. Explain the meaning and give examples of (a) physical safety, (b) legal safety, (c) mental safety, and (d) social-emotional safety.
2. What protection needs exist in your community?
3. List the steps your community could take in developing a protection program to meet the need you just identified.

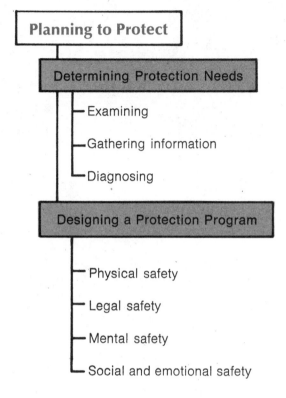

Planning to Protect

Determining Protection Needs

- Examining
- Gathering information
- Diagnosing

Designing a Protection Program

- Physical safety
- Legal safety
- Mental safety
- Social and emotional safety

Providing Welfare Services to Protect Children

Sad newspaper headlines such as these appear nearly every day in some part of the United States. While the details may differ from story to story, the real problem remains the same. A child in trouble needs help.

The love and understanding of a protection worker can help a disappointed, unhappy child build a new and better life.

Help for the child in trouble begins when adults try to understand his or her need for protection. They examine, gather information, and diagnose the problem. Using this knowledge, adults then plan to protect the child through a program that is designed to meet the child's needs. The programs may deal with physical, legal, mental, social, or emotional safety for the child. In the final step, welfare services are provided that, hopefully, can result in a normal, happy life for the child. .

While each member of a community shares the responsibility of protecting children, certain adults **specialize** in this work. Their education and training may be in law, social work, law enforcement, or child care. These specialists may work as a judge in a courtroom, a social worker at a children and family service department, a police officer patrolling the city, or a foster parent. They provide protection in many different forms to many different children. Most importantly, protection workers are helping improve young lives. They are often the only positive forces that ever enter a troubled child's existence.

THE CHILDREN

Most communities have children who are in trouble. Although their problems are often quite different, these children can be divided into three groups that are protected by welfare services. The three groups are these:

- **Dependent children**. These children are dependent upon society for total protection. Many dependent children are orphans. They may have been born without homes or may have lost their parents early in life. Dependent children can be of any age from infant to teen-ager.

- **Neglected children.** For many different reasons, parents sometimes neglect or ignore the protection needs of their children. Neglected children may have been beaten, denied enough food, forced to live in an unclean environment, or simply abandoned. About a century ago, the streets of many cities in the United States were filled with gangs of abandoned children who survived by stealing. Since welfare services have been established, the neglected and abused child receives care and protection.

- **Delinquent children.** Some children do not adjust as members of society. They may steal, cause damage to schools, or hurt other people physically. These are "delinquent" children. They must learn how to change their pattern of behavior. Education that helps these children learn to be more responsible for their behavior is often provided through the efforts of child welfare agencies.

Public and private child welfare agencies have many different programs that provide for the protection needs of these children.

What is the best type of protection for the child who is dependent? Neglected? Delinquent?

CHILD WELFARE AGENCY PROGRAMS

Child welfare agencies provide programs that can help solve problems in these ways:

1. Assist parents in home management.
2. Arrange adoptions for homeless infants and children.
3. Protect neglected or abused children.
4. Place in the hands of specialists those children who suffer from serious physical, mental, or emotional-social problems.

Within just one week, the child welfare agency might provide programs to such people as those whose problems are described below:

A young mother is having great difficulty in managing and caring for her large family. She calls the child welfare agency and asks for help. The agency carefully interviews the mother to learn the facts that cause her problem. The agency then studies the case to determine how its services can help the mother solve her problems. It decides to send a **homemaker's aide** to the mother's home. The homemaker's aide shows the woman how to plan inexpensive but tasty, well-balanced meals; manage money for food and rent; and organize her day so that she is able to give her children the care and attention they need to grow up and become happy, healthy adults.

Four-year-old Pam is **being abused and neglected** in her natural home. A social worker calls at Pam's home and gathers information about the child and her environment. He or she may recommend that special help be given to the family to improve the environment and child care practices. If the social worker feels that it would be impossible to improve the situation, he or she may recommend that Pam be removed from the home. The social worker then appears in court and receives permission to remove the child. This is done **only** if no solution to the home problems can be found. Pam may be assigned to a foster home chosen by the agency. The husband and wife who offer the foster home will give Pam love and good care.

With the assistance of a homemaker's aide, a mother may learn to manage meals and other housework responsibilities more efficiently.

If a home environment cannot be improved, then the social worker may recommend assigning a child to foster parents and a new environment.

Billy, age 14, is always in trouble. The court asks the agency to help him. A social worker from the agency talks to Billy, his parents, and others who are concerned in the case. It is determined that his parents can no longer give him the special care and guidance he needs. The social worker reviews the facts of Billy's case in a conference with the other social workers. They decide that Billy's special needs can best be met in an institution staffed with specialists. The social worker asks the court to send Billy to a special **corrective home** for boys where he can receive help.

Tom is a very slow learner. His first grade teacher recommends that Tom receive help from a child welfare agency. The agency has Tom tested by a psychologist. The psychologist asks Tom questions and has him perform simple tasks with his hands. Tom is discovered to be mildly retarded. The agency aid's Tom's parents in entering the child in a special day school for retarded children.

Jane, age 3, spends each day in a day care center while her mother works. Although the day care center has a good program and a staff that cares

about each child, the outside play area is no longer safe. An inspector from the Department of Children and Family Services visits the day care center to

The social worker may recommend a special school to help a child with severe learning problems.

When a child needs special corrective help, the social worker may recommend an institution staffed with experienced specialists who are trained to help children solve their problems.

Day care centers provide for the protection needs of children and give their mothers confidence while they are working or absent from their children.

inspect the program and facilities, as the center wishes to renew it's state operating license. The inspector informs the director of the center that a new fence must be built around the play area to protect the children from traffic. To continue to provide its services to children and to obtain a license renewal, the director arranges for a new fence to be built.

ADOPTION AGENCY PROGRAMS

The **adoption agency** offers a program that protects everyone involved in the adoption of homeless children. Mother, infant, and the adopting couple are served by social workers, aides, and the agency supervisor. If this is a public agency (operated by the state welfare department), a district administrator and office manager are also members of the team offering adoption services. Just how does this program meet the protection needs of dependent children?

Most homeless children, called "waiting children," are handicapped, racially mixed, or past the infant stage in age. Waiting children may be cared for in institutions or foster homes until a suitable, permanent home can be found. A foster home must be approved by both the state and the adoption agency. Children of all ages can be placed in foster homes.

The entire process of adoption can be examined in the following story of how an infant named Holly found a home through the adoption agency. Holly, who lived in a state-approved (licensed) foster home, is an exception in modern adoption. Infants being available for adoption is rare today.

Holly's mother was unmarried and had placed Holly up for adoption when the infant was 72 hours old. After the court gave the adoption agency custody of Holly, the agency temporarily placed her in a foster home. A search was then started to find new permanent parents that would provide a healthy environment for the child.

A picture of Holly was placed in the agency's special book that lists all the children available for adoption. Beneath the picture was information describing Holly,

The court awards custody of a young child to the adoption agency. As the social worker accepts the judgment, she is also accepting the responsibility of finding a suitable home for the child.

The adoption agency prepares a page of information on an adoptable child, showing a photo and listing the background, age, health, and other personal characteristics of the child.

including her background, personal characteristics, and state of health. In another section, the adoptive listing book also listed the names and information about families wanting to adopt children from the agency. The listing described the kind of children each family wanted to adopt. Social workers at the agency studied the book, trying to find the right parents for Holly.

A couple named Webster seemed to qualify as adoptive parents. Mr. and Mrs. Webster hoped to adopt an infant, preferably a girl. They were eager to offer love, good care, and a comfortable home. A social worker investigated the Websters carefully. Either she or a trained case aide visited their home and interviewed them several times. They seemed the kind of people who would give Holly affection and understanding and would provide for her needs. The social worker checked the personal references the Websters had listed. She also examined their financial situation. The Websters did not need to be wealthy, but they did have to be able to provide for Holly's material needs. The social worker wrote down all these facts in her case study, a report explaining the progress of the case.

The social worker showed Holly's picture to the Websters and told them about her. Later, at the agency, the couple met Holly. Both of the Websters wanted little Holly for their own. The social worker and the agency committee recommended that Holly should be placed in the Webster home. Soon after this, the Websters and their lawyer went to court and filed a petition for adoption. After six months a final decree was issued by the court. It made Holly a legal member of the Webster family. She received a new birth certificate listing the Websters as her legal parents. The old birth certificate was put into confidential court records.

Introducing the child to her new home and new parents is a delicate procedure which the social worker must plan carefully.

One of the social worker's duties in preparing her case study is to interview prospective parents to discover what kind of home they can provide for an adopted child.

Permanent parents, carefully chosen by the agency, will provide for the child's material needs, but, above all, will offer love and the security of a family environment.

The adoption agency had found Holly a home. She would receive protection, love, affection, and the security of a family. She would have a chance to develop into a happy, productive member of society. Having Holly as a family member fulfilled the Webster's desire for a child they could call their own. Not only does the adoption agency's service benefit the child and the family, but it also benefits the community. By having a permanent home environment, the child is more capable of adjusting to society and becoming a responsible member of the community.

LAW AND ENFORCEMENT PROGRAMS

The protection needs of children are also met through the programs of **law** and **enforcement**. Law and enforcement are sometimes thought of as concerned mainly with police. However, police only make up a small part of the protection program. In addition to police, law and enforcement is composed of the courts, probation departments, correction institutions, parole boards, and those who make our laws — state legislators and members of Congress.

This sign, warning motorists that children cross the street at this point, is an example of how law enforcement designs to protect children.

Below is a law enacted by the government of the state of Illinois. It is called The Abused Child Act. Read this law carefully. One of the most important elements of this law is that it requires responsible adults to report suspected cases of child abuse to the proper authorities. This kind of program ensures that abused children will be protected from their unsafe environment.

The Abused Child Act

AN ACT for the reporting of certain cases of physical abuse, neglect or injury to children, and to make an appropriation in connection therewith. Approved March 31, 1965, as amended.

Section 1. Unless the context otherwise requires: "child" means any person under the age of 16 years, "Department" means the Department of Children and Family Services, "local law enforcement agency" means the police of a city, town, village or other incorporated area or the sheriff of an unincorporated area.

Section 2. Any physician, surgeon, dentist, osteopath, chiropractor, podiatrist or Christian Science practitioner having reasonable cause to believe that a child brought to him or coming before him for examination, care or treatment, or any school teacher, school administrator, truant officer, social worker, social service administrator, registered nurse, licensed practical nurse, director or staff assistant of a nursery school or child day care center, law enforcement officer, or field personnel of the Illinois Department of Public Aid or the Cook County Department of Public Aid having reasonable cause to believe that any child with whom they have direct contact has suffered injury or disability from physical abuse, or neglect inflicted upon him or shows evidence of malnutrition, other than by accidental means, or has been subjected to deliberate withholding of feeding endangering his health, and any hospital to which a child comes or is brought suffering from injury, physical abuse, or neglect apparently inflicted upon him or shows evidence of malnutrition, other than by accidental means, shall promptly report or cause reports to be made in accordance with this Act. This Section applies to cases of children whose death occurs from apparent injury, neglect or malnutrition, other than by accidental means, before being found or brought to a hospital. A child whose parent, guardian or custodian in good faith selects and depends upon spiritual means through prayer alone for the treatment or cure of disease or remedial care may be considered neglected or abused, but not for the sole reason that his parent, guardian, or custodian accepts and practices the aforementioned beliefs.

Section 3. The report required by this Act shall be made immediately by phone or in person to the nearest office of the Department; and shall also be made in writing deposited in the U. S. mail, postage prepaid, within 24 hours after having reasonable cause to believe that the condition of the child results from physical abuse or neglect. The Department shall initiate an investigation of each report of child abuse under this Act, whether oral or written, within 24 hours after the receipt of such report. This investigation shall include but not be limited by an onsite investigation at the residence of the abused child. The Department may delegate to other public agencies or to private social services agencies the performance of the onsite investigation. Such reports may in addition be made to the local law enforcement agency in the same manner. In the event a report is made to the local law enforcement agency, the reporter shall so inform the Department.

(The Act continues with further provisions.)

Now read the newspaper article. A suspected case of child abuse was reported. The father of an infant was found guilty in court and sentenced to prison. Because of law and enforcement, the infant may have the chance to grow and develop into a healthy, happy adult.

LINCOLN MAN FACES ABUSE COUNT

LINCOLN — Leonard Violent, 21, Monday was arrested on a battery charge in connection with the alleged mistreatment of his 10-month-old stepdaughter, Anna, on Sunday.

A complaint, charging battery signed by the child's mother, has been issued in magistrate division of circuit court.

BEATING RESULTS IN FINE AND PRISON

LINCOLN — Leonard Violent, 21, of Lincoln was sentenced in circuit court Monday to six months at the State Penal Farm at Vandalia and fined $500 after being found guilty of battery.

Violent was charged with beating his 10-month-old step-daughter, Anna, with his hands and a belt and with inflicting cigarette burns on her body and feet on Oct. 22.

Judge Robert Fairness stressed that this is the maximum penalty provided by law for battery. Violent was denied probation.

OTHER PROGRAMS

On the federal level, safety experts for the Consumer Product Safety Commission check toys sold in stores to protect children from materials that can prove harmful. Toy safety is also enforced by state and local departments. Thousands of toys are banned by these agencies and are often withdrawn from the market voluntarily by toy manufacturers. These protection programs save many young eyes and bodies from serious damage. Look at these "ten command-

ments" for toy safety. If followed, would they offer good protection to children?

Ten Commandments for Toy Safety

The following "ten commandments" that offer protection for children should be observed when making toy purchases.

1. A good toy shall not cut, gouge, have sharp or pointed edges or glass parts.
2. A good toy shall not catch or pinch fingers, clothes, or flesh.
3. A good toy shall not burn, include combustible material, or have exposed surfaces that reach high temperatures.
4. A good toy shall not explode or make loud noises that could result in permanent hearing loss.
5. A good toy shall not come apart into small pieces that can be swallowed.
6. A good toy shall not shock or, if designed for small children, use more than 120 volts of electricity. (Look for UL — Underwriters Laboratories — labels on the cords and body of the toy.)
7. A good toy shall include no ropes or loops that can strangle.
8. A good toy shall not have rough, unfinished surfaces or toxic paints or dyes.
9. A good toy shall have no suction tips that come off, revealing sharp points beneath.
10. No small child shall have a toy for unsupervised use that shoots a projectile.

Remember these pointers:

- Broken toys can be hazardous. Throw them out.
- Toys should be selected that are appropriate for a child's age and development.
- Check instructions — any toy can cause injury through misuse.
- Check fabric labels for flame resistance.

Remember, a toy is only as safe as its owner.

Many schools offer **rehabilitation and counseling** programs for handicapped children and students. The blind, deaf, or lame child must be protected from harm by learning to overcome or adjust to the handicap.

Such children must learn how to deal with their handicap on a physical level through training by physical therapists or teachers of special education. Also, they must overcome mental and emotional side effects of the handicap, such as shyness or depression.

Children may be protected by **residential care programs.** The chart below shows how the number of children living in training schools for juvenile delinquents has increased over a ten-year-period. Not only must their formal education continue, but the educational programs must also help them discover why they acted in a delinquent manner. Psychologists, clergy, and teachers attempt to help these children achieve a better concept of themselves and

Persons in Custody in Training Schools for Juvenile Delinquents and in Detention Homes: 1960 and 1970

Characteristic	1960				1970			
	Training Schools for Juvenile Delinquents			Detention Homes	Training Schools for Juvenile Delinquents			Detention Homes
	Total	Public	Private		Total	Public	Private	
Total	45,695	38,359	7,336	10,821	66,457	57,691	8,766	10,272
Male	33,765	29,681	4,084	7,680	52,769	46,867	5,902	6,590
Female	11,930	8,678	3,252	3,141	13,688	10,824	2,864	3,682
White	31,294	24,900	6,394	7,342	39,757	33,428	6,329	6,754
Negro and other	14,401	13,459	942	3,479	26,700	24,263	2,437	3,518
Under 10 years old	476	327	149	785	1,006	647	359	481
10-13 years old	6,131	4,858	1,273	2,468	7,291	5,581	1,710	1,986
14 years old	6,078	5,067	1,011	1,625	8,272	6,873	1,399	1,656
15-19 years old	31,316	26,676	4,640	4,988	42,767	37,929	4,838	5,937
20 years old and over	1,694	1,431	263	955	7,121	6,661	460	212

(1960 based on 25-percent sample, 1970 on 20-percent sample. Comparability of figures is affected by differences in classification.)

Source: U.S. Bureau of the Census, U.S. Census of Population: 1960, and 1970, vol. II.

Organized activities in a residential care facility are designed to help change young troubled children into productive responsible ones.

their place in the world. Physical education programs develop their young bodies. Many of these schools teach older children useful skills they can use to earn a living.

Dependent, neglected, and delinquent children are all served by protection pro-

grams. By protecting their normal growth and development, environment, and helping change situations that cause behavior problems, public and private agencies can help change troubled young lives into productive, happy ones.

REVIEWING YOUR VOCABULARY

abandoned
positive force
existence
dependent children
neglected children
delinquent children
home management
homemaker's aide
conference
corrective home
day school

administrator
law and enforcement
probation
 departments
correction
 institutions
parole boards
abused child act
depressions
residential care
 programs

INCREASING YOUR PERCEPTION

1. Identify the types of children who may use the services of a protective agency.
2. Describe types of protection services offered by (a) child welfare agencies, (b) adoption agencies, (c) law and enforcement, (d) rehabilitation and counseling, and (e) residential care.
3. What types of protective services might you use? What type of child would you be if you used the services in that way?

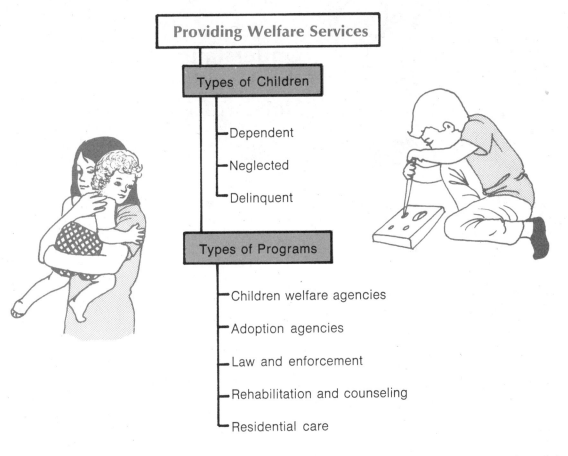

Providing Welfare Services

Types of Children

- Dependent
- Neglected
- Delinquent

Types of Programs

- Children welfare agencies
- Adoption agencies
- Law and enforcement
- Rehabilitation and counseling
- Residential care

Reading15

Understanding the Health Care Needs of Children

Understanding the health care needs of children has been a major concern of people for many years. From Hippocrates, who first based medical treatment on scientific examination about 400 B.C., to Christian Barnard, who performed the first successful heart transplant in 1967, **the medical profession has attempted to understand and cure disease.**

Great progress has been made. Not so very long ago, many babies died before their first birthday. The **mortality rate** (the number of children who did not reach adulthood) was very high. Before this century, very few records of mortality rates were kept, and therefore, the exact mortality rate was not known. After people became more conscious of children's health care, they started

Infant, Maternal, Fetal, and Neonatal Death Rates: 1940 to 1971
(Deaths per 1,000 live births, except as noted. Prior to 1960, excludes Alaska and Hawaii.)

Item	1940	1950	1955	1960	1965	1966	1967	1968	1969 (prel.)	1970 (prel.)	1971 (prel.)
Infant deaths [1]	47.0	29.2	26.4	26.0	24.7	23.7	22.4	21.8	20.7	19.8	19.2
Maternal deaths [2]	376.0	83.3	47.0	37.1	31.6	29.1	28.0	24.5	27.4	24.7	20.5
Fetal deaths [3]	(NA)	19.2	17.1	16.1	16.2	15.7	15.6	15.8	(NA)	(NA)	(NA)
Neonatal deaths [4]	28.8	20.5	19.1	18.7	17.7	17.2	16.5	16.1	15.4	14.9	14.3

NA Not available.

1 Represents deaths of infants under 1 year old, exclusive of fetal deaths.

2 Per 100,000 live births from deliveries and complications of pregnancy, childbirth, and the puerperium.

3 Includes only fetal deaths (stillbirths) for which period of gestation was 20 weeks (or 5 months) or more, or was not stated.

4 Represents deaths of infants under 28 days old, exclusive of fetal deaths.

SOURCE: U. S. Public Health Service, Vital Statistics of the United States, annual.

Records, such as mortality rates, help researchers identify problems that, if solved, improve human living conditions.

keeping such records. In 1900, **162 of every 1000 babies died** before living one year. In 1950, the rate had dropped to **29 of every 1000.** In 1970, only about **20 of every 1000 babies** died before their first birthday! What caused this great decrease?

Because records were kept, people realized how many infants did not live. Doctors and scientists tried to understand the reasons for infant deaths. Through **examinations** and **health data** (information that was compiled), they discovered that poor care of the mother before birth, poor food for babies, and unclean environments were causing the high infant mortality rate. Once the medical profession understood and worked toward infant health care needs, the mortality rate dropped.

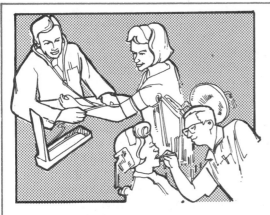

A complete physical examination and a checkup by the doctor and dentist are important steps in determining the present health of an expectant mother.

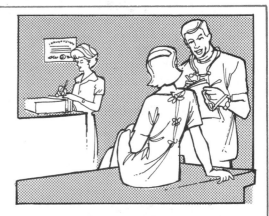

The maternity doctor compiles data by asking the patient questions about her health and her present state of mind.

After the maternity doctor has studied the information gathered from the examination and the medical history, he will discuss the findings with his patient and her husband. Together they will work out a prescription for health care during pregnancy.

Throughout pregnancy, examinations continue and records are kept on the health of both the mother and unborn child.

Through examinations and study of compiled health data, parents and health care workers are able to care for children even before they are born.

Today adults understand much about the health care needs of their children and are constantly learning more. Adults now realize that health care is not something required only by children who are ill. Children must receive health care **every day** of their lives.

CHILDREN'S HEALTH CARE NEEDS

Health care is much more than taking a child to a doctor if illness occurs. Children must have their health care needs met **every day** in order to grow and develop normally. Through daily care, adults hope to prevent major illnesses that could have **long-term** effects on their children.

Latest flu bug hits mainly at children

Such diseases as influenza (flu) can often infect many children in a community. They must be treated promptly and effectively.

What kind of health care do children need? First of all, they need to be free from **disease.** A disease, such as **pneumonia,** can infect children's lungs. **Leukemia** is a disease of the blood that often attacks children. **Chicken pox** and **measles** are common childhood diseases that also can be very serious. Another common disease called **influenza** (flu), if not properly treated, can harm a child and even cause death.

Children also need to be free from **bodily injury** — broken bones, cuts, and sprains. Because children are every active, they fall and injure themselves more often than adults. If not cared for properly, a simple little cut can become infected and lead to a serious health problem. **Burns** are especially dangerous. As they explore, toddlers may pull a scalding hot pan down from the stove and cause serious burns to themselves.

Not all health care needs are physical. Children have **mental health needs** too. Children can become frightened, depressed, angry, withdrawn, and confused just as adults do. If the child is frightened all the time, a mental health problem may exist. Children enjoying good mental health usually do not have these traits for long periods of time.

Children must feel that they are accepted by other children their own age. This is an important part of **social-emotional** health. Children need to feel that they are important members of their families. They must have good relationships with others both in and out of the home if they are to develop good feelings about themselves.

Children's health care needs begin as soon as life itself begins. The better the health of the mother, the better chance the newborn has for good health. As children grow and develop, adults must continually check the child's health care needs. Even the most rosy-cheeked, active child can become ill if disease, injury, or behavior problems are not discovered and treated. The process of discovering and treating health problems begins when adults examine health care needs.

RULES FOR GOOD HEALTH

1. EAT A BALANCED DIET

For growth and energy your body needs milk, meat eggs, fruits, vegetables, breads, and cereals.

2. EXERCISE DAILY

This develops your muscles, keeps your blood circulating, and helps you keep your proper weight.

3. REST AND RELAX

Your body needs sleep to repair tissue and keep away disease. Your mind, too, needs to relax and be free from tension.

4. SEE YOUR DOCTOR & DENTIST

They help you to guard your health. Brushing your teeth daily, and keeping your body clean, will also help stop illness from beginning.

5. KEEP YOUR ENVIRONMENT CLEAN

Germs love dirt. By keeping your home, school, and play areas clean you will help keep germs away!

6. KEEP YOUR ENVIRONMENT SAFE

Follow safety rules wherever you are.

Don't play in dangerous areas.

7. ENJOY LIFE!

Have fun when you work and play. You need the feeling of pleasure, the joy of laughter, and the chance to be just plain silly.

8. THINK POSITIVE

Positive thoughts can produce positive actions. Belief in a religion or philosophy will help you be positive in your thinking.

EXAMINING HEALTH CARE NEEDS

Adults examine the health care needs of children in these ways:

- Listening
- Touching
- Looking

Examining a child is done by parents in the home and by medical specialists, such as doctors, outside the home. Examining reveals either that a child's health needs are being met or that certain problems exist.

Problems show up as **symptoms** (signs). Sore throats, headaches, high temperature, or difficulty in breathing are all symptoms of illness. When adults examine children, they look for symptoms.

REVIEWING MEDICAL HISTORY

The first step in examining is **reviewing medical history** or looking into the child's past health. Parents may review by simply remembering what illnesses little Mary or Johnny have had and how a cure was brought about. Medical specialists review in a more formal way. Doctors and dentists keep a medical file on each patient. This file contains a history of past illnesses and treatments. Each illness, operation, accident, injury, and treatment is carefully listed. By looking at this history, the medical worker has a better understanding of the patient.

A health history card is used by dentists. When the dentist examines a child, a look at the card informs the dentist of the type of problems the patient has had in the past. Your dentist probably has a card somewhat like this for you.

LISTENING TO THE BODY

After reviewing medical history, adults examine children by **listening**. Your body

---

CHILD'S MEDICAL HISTORY

(These questions are of value to us in understanding your child.)

A. Child's Name.................................... Nickname........................

B. Age............ Birthday.................... Place of Birth.....................

CHECK ONE:
YES NO

C. Is your child in good health?.................... ☐ ☐

D. Does your child have regular medical examinations? ☐ ☐

E. Has your child any history of heart trouble, allergies, diabetes, asthma, kidney or liver involvement, epilepsy, bleeding disorder or brain injury? (If answer is ye_ _____ condition.)..................... ☐ ☐

F. Ha_ _____ rebral or spastic condition?......... ☐ ☐

G. Ha_ _____ normal mental condition? ... ☐ ☐

H. Ha_ _____ ious Fluoride treatme_ ☐ ☐

I. Has _ _____ ced any unfavor_ _ from _ _____ medical _ ☐ ☐

J. Is your _ _____ ☐ ☐

K. Is you_ _____ ☐ ☐

L. Giv_ _____

W_ _____

R_ _____

Medical workers use the information on medical history records to gain a better understanding of the patient.

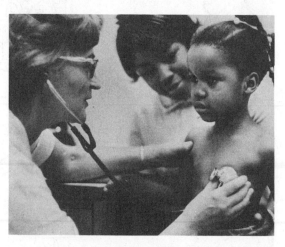

By using a stethoscope, the doctor can listen to a child's heartbeat or other body sounds.

talks, you know! Your heart and lungs have a certain sound when operating normally. By using an instrument called a **stethoscope,** doctors can listen to the body's sounds.

TOUCHING THE BODY

Examining continues by **touching.** When children tell their parents that they do not feel well, parents often touch their children's foreheads with their hands. Very warm skin could be a symptom of high temperature. Doctors touch children as they examine their muscles or take their **pulse** (count the throbs in a blood vessel to determine the heart beat). Dentists touch as they examine children's teeth for cavities.

Testing reflexes is a special part of touching. A reflex is a physical response that you cannot ordinarily control. (It is an involuntary act.) In testing reflexes, doctors may tap children on a nerve beneath the kneecap with a small neurological hammer. This causes the leg to jerk. Another reflex often tested by doctors is the blinking of a patient's eyelid when a light is flashed into the eye. The purpose of these tests is to discover any problems with muscles or the central nervous system.

LOOKING AT THE BODY

The examination continues when a parent or specialist **looks** at the child's body. When the eye specialist (ophthalmologist) examines children's eyes, a special instrument called an **ophthalmoscope** is used. This instrument lights up and magnifies the inside of the eyeball. The doctor can then clearly see the optic disc (where the nerve enters the eye from the brain), the blood vessels, and the back of the inside eyeball called the **retina.**

Parents **look** at their children often to see whether they appear alert, happy, and in good physical condition. A child's skin is a good indicator of health. If it suddenly develops red spots or feels very warm to the touch, parents know that the child is becoming ill. If a child suddenly begins to lose weight, squint, limp, or show other symptoms, parents become aware of a possible health problem.

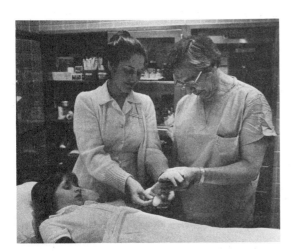

By gently touching the arm, the doctor examines the bone for fractures (breaks).

In examining the child, the doctor looks at parts of the body where symptoms of illness may be present.

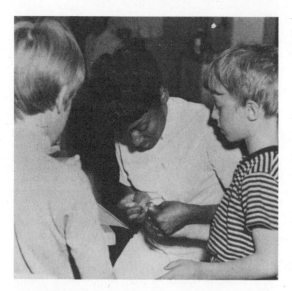

Sometimes blood tests are conducted in community clinics that visit schools and other public places to examine large numbers of children at one time.

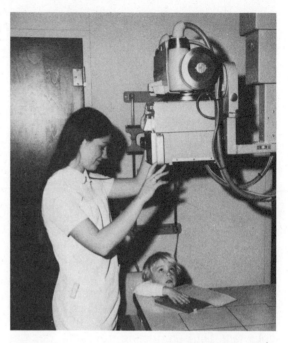

An X-ray technician "photographs" bones and organs to aid the doctor in the diagnosis and treatment of his patient.

TESTING

During examination, **testing** is sometimes required. For example, an examination may reveal symptoms of a disease such as **thalassemia.** Children suffering from this disease may show such symptoms as listlessness, pale skin, and constant infection of some kind. Usually growth and development are slow. This blood disease usually affects people with Mediterranean, Near Eastern, or Southern Asiatic ancestry. There are about 250,000 people in the United States who could pass this disease on to their children. When a doctor suspects that a child may have thalassemia, a **blood test** is ordered. A sample of the child's blood is taken and examined. In this way, the disease can be identified.

The **X-ray** is another type of test. The X-ray machine can take a picture of the inside of the body. X-rays help a physician examine broken or fractured bones. Damage to the head, eye, and organs of a child's body can also be identified by an X-ray test. Sometimes children swallow dangerous ob-jects, such as an open safety pin. By examining an X-ray of the child's stomach, the doctor can tell what was swallowed and how dangerous it will be to the child.

COMPILING HEALTH DATA

During the examination, much information is often discovered. This information must be recorded in some way so that it can be retrieved in the future. The most common method of recording health care information is to write it down. The information is then compiled according to (1) subject, (2) content, or (3) purpose. This type of classification is a way of organizing information into an understandable form.

A parent, for example, might want to compile information about the **immunization** of each child in the family. Immunization provides protection against certain diseases

Immunization Record

NAME Kevin R. Jones

	DATE	DOSE	PHYSICIAN
POLIOMYELITIS (Inactivated vaccine, Salk)	3·2·68	Sane 1	[signature]
	4·3·68	2	[signature]
	5·8·68	SmBR3	[signature]
POLIOMYELITIS (OPV, Sabin)	6·6·69	2	[signature]
	6·19·73	SmB.2	WBaler
MEASLES (Live attenuated virus) (Live attenuated virus plus immune globulin)			
MEASLES (Inactivated vaccine) *Mumps –*	2·15·70	Rubindex	[signature]
	2·2·70	mumps	[signature]
MEASLES COMBINED SCHEDULE — Inactivated (Inactivated and live attenuated vaccines) — Live virus			
COMBINED DTP (Diphtheria, tetanus, pertussis) *6-19-73*	3·2·68	DP +1	[signature]
	4·3·68	2	[signature]
	5·8·68	P3	[signature]
	6·6·69		[signature]
COMBINED DT (Diphtheria, tetanus, adult type)			
TETANUS			
DIPHTHERIA			
PERTUSSIS			

	DATE	MATERIAL	METHOD	RESULT	PHYSICIAN
SMALLPOX	10·26·68			Primary	[signature]
TUBERCULIN	7·20·68			Tine	
OTHER					

Records like this help parents and health care specialists organize important information about a child's health.

and is given in the form of shots. The parent can bring a card, such as the one on this page, to the family doctor. The doctor examines his or her own records and records this information on the card. The parent can then tell at a glance what immunization the child has had and what kind will be needed in the future.

As dentists examine children's teeth, they must record and compile the important information they discover. A child may have three cavities in three separate teeth and some signs of decay beginning to form in another tooth. The dentist must have a record of the findings for present and future appointments with the patient.

This dental chart shows top and side views of a child's teeth. Dentists use this chart to mark the location of each cavity or dental problem. In the future, the dentist can review a child's dental history by referring to the chart.

Through **examining and compiling,** parents and health care specialists are able

---

NAME **Kevin R. Jones**   AGE **6**   SEX **M**

PERSON RESPONSIBLE FOR ACCT. **R SCOTT JONES**   RES. PHONE **495-6132**

BUS. PHONE **662-1465**

RES. ADDRESS **2313 E Monroe, Normal Ill.** ZIP CODE **61761**

BUS. ADDRESS **309 MAIN, NORMAL, Ill.** ZIP CODE **61761**

EMPLOYED BY **ABC Products Ltd.** DUTIES **Designer**

REFERRED BY **Ken Johnson, DDS - OLDE TOWNE** MARITAL STATUS **Married**

REMARKS **Continue treatment begun by Dr. Johnson.**

RESTORATION & ESTIMATE

TEETH	DESCRIPTION	FEE
L14	O-dy amal SNF2	5—
LI	O-dy amal SNF2	5—
LⅠ	O-dy amal SNF2	10—
IK	MO-dy amal SNF2 (deep)	10—
IL	O-dy amal SNF2	5—
I19	O-dy amal SNF2	5—
BI	O-dy amal SNF2	5—
BⅠ	O-dy amal SNF2	5—
AI	O-dy amal SNF2	5—
30I	Of-dy amal SNF2	10—
5I	O-dy amal SNF2	10—
FI	O-dy amal SNF2	5—

a b c d e   f g h i   j
V IV III II I   I II III IV V

E   D C B A A B C D   E
t   s r q p o n m l   k

X-Rays **Full series**

Date **1/14/74**

Study Model _____

Photograph _____

Transillumination Area _____

UPPER

RIGHT   LEFT

LOWER

MARK H. LOWELL D.D.S.

DOCTOR'S PARK - BLOOMINGTON, ILL.

When a family moves to another town, records like this will help their new dentist to continue a program of dental care.

to gain a better understanding of children's complete health needs. By giving careful thought to the compiled information, adults can reach a decision as to a child's state of health. This decision is called a **diagnosis**. You will learn more about diagnosing in Reading 16.

REVIEWING YOUR VOCABULARY

Hippocrates	chicken pox	testing reflexes
treatment	measles	ophthalmologist
scientific	influenza	ophthalmoscope
heart transplant	bodily injury	thalassemia
mortality rate	depressed	blood test
maternal	withdrawn	X-ray
fetal	symptoms	immunizations
neonatal	medical history	cavity
long term	stethoscope	decay
pneumonia	pulse	diagnosis
leukemia		

INCREASING YOUR PERCEPTION

1. Describe health care needs of infants, toddlers, preschoolers, and elementary children.
2. Give examples of different ways a child may be examined to determine his or her state of health.
3. Identify medical records that should be kept for each child.

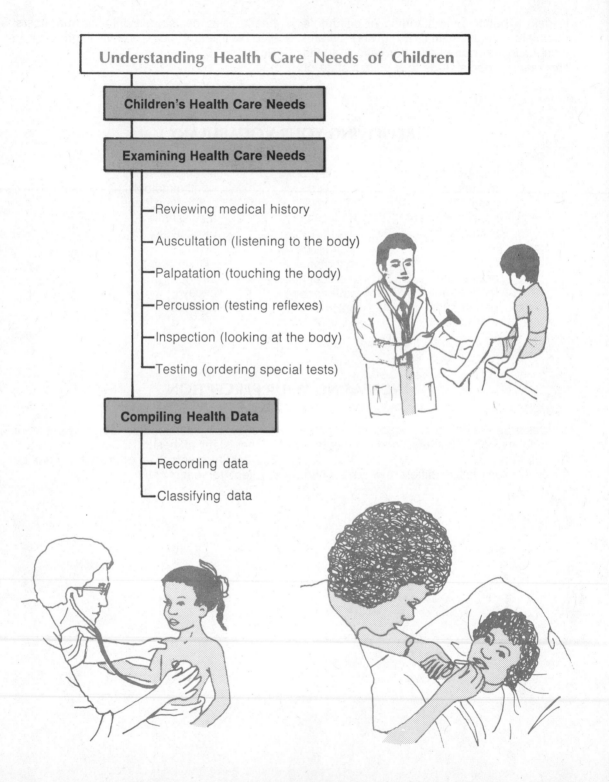

Understanding Health Care Needs of Children

Children's Health Care Needs

Examining Health Care Needs

— Reviewing medical history

— Auscultation (listening to the body)

— Palpatation (touching the body)

— Percussion (testing reflexes)

— Inspection (looking at the body)

— Testing (ordering special tests)

Compiling Health Data

— Recording data

— Classifying data

Diagnosing and Prescribing to Meet Children's Health Care Needs

At the eye clinic, the doctor finished her examination of the 10-year-old boy. The findings discovered during examination had all been recorded and compiled. The doctor carefully considered the recorded information and then wrote her **diagnosis** (conclusion) on a card. The diagnosis was that the little boy had a severe case of **myopia** (nearsightedness). This meant that because of the shape of the boy's eyeball, he could only see objects clearly that were close to him.

"What's going to happen now?" asked the boy.

"I am going to **prescribe** glasses for you," answered the doctor. "In about a year, I will examine your eyes again. If the examination shows that you need stronger lenses in your glasses, I will prescribe them for you."

Parents and health care workers, such as the **eye doctor** (ophthalmologist), compare their knowledge of a normal child's state of health to the information gathered from the examination. This information is then used to diagnose (determine) the need for health care and to prescribe a treatment. Diagnosing is a process of **(1) identifying a condition or disease and (2) determining the cause or nature of the illness.** Prescribing involves (1) **directing a medical treatment of some kind,** such as giving medicine; (2) **directing an instructional action,** such as teaching a child not to touch fire; or (3) **directing a rehabilitating action,** such as one that would enable a child to learn to walk again. Parents often consult a specialist if they lack the knowledge to prescribe the correct action themselves.

PARENTS DIAGNOSE AND PRESCRIBE

Parents are usually more involved with children's day-to-day health care needs than anybody else. It is often the parent who first becomes aware that a child is in need of health care and decides what action will best meet that need.

Parents diagnose and prescribe in many ways. For example, a fever may be diagnosed when a child's temperature is taken with a thermometer. A prescription might include rest in bed and a call to the doctor for a more thorough examination, diagnosis, and prescription.

 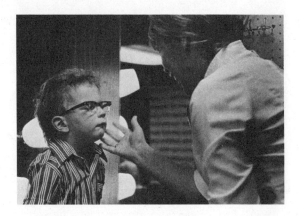

NAME *Don Doe*

AGE *8* OCCUPATION *Student*

EMPLOYER —

REFERRED BY *Dr. T. E. Morgan*

ADD. *123 Main St.*
Hometown, Illinois 61000

DATE *5-5-74*

	VISION		WITH GLASSES	
	OD 20/400		OD 20/80	
	OS 20/400		OS 20/70	

HISTORY *- Routine -*
Present Rx 1 yr.
No Problems
No known drug allergies
Health good - No injuries
or surgery - Worn
glasses 6 yrs. - Wear
constantly, thinks
glasses need changing -
Having difficulty seeing
blackboard clearly -

WEARS   OD *- 6.00 - 1.75 x 90*
OS *- 6.50 - 2.00 x 78*

MANIFEST OD *- 6.75 - 1.75 x 90* *20/20*
OS *- 6.50 - 2.00 x 78* *20/20*

RETINOSCOPY (dynamic—static)
OD *- 7.00 - 1.50 x 90*
OS *- 6.50 - 2.00 x 78*

CYCLOPLEGIC ACCEPTANCE
OD
OS

PRESCRIPTION
OD *- 6.75 - 1.75 x 90*
OS *- 6.50 - 2.00 x 78*

DIAGNOSIS *Myopia OU*

FUNDUS *OU - Normal*

ADVISED: *Healthy eyes -*
Change in glasses
needed.

QUOTATION

FINDINGS:
Versions & pupils -
Normal

Slit lamp - Corneas
clear except
for a few small
pigmented KP's

The ophthalmologist (eye doctor) examines his patient's eyes, evaluates his recorded findings, and diagnoses a health care need. A prescription for glasses is then prepared to meet that need.

DIAGNOSING AND PRESCRIBING FOR PHYSICAL ILLNESS

A young mother named Betty made a diagnosis and used a prescription for action that could have saved her four-year-old son's life. One summer morning little Billy, who had been playing in the neighborhood, returned home very ill. He was vomiting. At first, his mother wondered whether Billy was coming down with the flu or a cold, although he was not running a temperature. She asked if he had been injured. Billy shook his head no.

Betty undressed Billy and put him in bed. As she was hanging up his jacket, she felt something in a pocket. It was an old bottle of household cleanser. The bottle was half empty. Betty showed the bottle to Billy and asked him whether he had drank from it. He nodded yes. "I was playing drug store with Tommy," said Billy.

Billy had become one of about **500,000 children** under the age of five who suffer from poisoning each year. Fighting panic, Betty hurried to the telephone. Long ago, she had written this prescription for making emergency phone calls:

1. Have a pencil and paper next to the telephone to write down directions.
2. Have a special list of phone numbers of doctors, pharmacists, police, and other specialists.
3. Give the doctor or other health care worker your full name and address. Give the child's name and age.
4. Describe the health problem in simple, but detailed language. State all symptoms.

Betty checked her list of phone numbers and found one for the local **Poison Control Center.** This center had information about thousands of products and knew which products were poisonous. Betty described Billy's problem to the center's physician, giving him the product name on the old bottle. "He'll be fine," said the physician. "There should be no other effects other than the vomiting. However, you might call your family doctor and explain what happened."

Betty sat by the telephone for a moment, still trembling. She felt a tug at her arm.

"Mom," said Billy. "Can I go outside and play some more? I feel better now."

The following newspaper article offers a prescription for parents, telling them how to protect their children from poisoning. Someone in Billy's neighborhood might not have carelessly thrown out that old bottle of household cleanser if he or she had read this article. The bottle should have been destroyed.

Here's How to Avoid Childhood Poisonings

An estimated 500,000 children, most younger than 5 years of age, will accidentally swallow poisons in their homes this year. And about 400 of the victims will die as a result of these accidents.

Internal medicines, in tablet form, are responsible for most childhood poisonings. And though it sounds unlikely, it has been reported that aspirin is the substance most often involved.

Other common household chemicals that frequently cause accidental poisonings include cleaning fluids, detergents, petroleum distillates (lighter fluid, gasoline, and kerosene), paint and paint products, cosmetics, and pesticides.

Between 8,000 and 9,000 poisonings involving children less than 13 years of age are expected in Illinois this year. More than 95 per cent of the victims will be preschoolers, and most will be one- and two-year olds.

The curiosity of preschoolers makes them especially prone to accidents of this type because they like to mimic adults.

Here are some suggestions for parents to follow:

— Keep medicines out of reach and out of sight of young children.

— Store medicines in closed cabinets or chests that cannot be opened by very young children.

— Don't refer to medicines, such as flavored aspirin, as "candy."

— Always keep medications and other potential poisons properly labeled and in their original containers.

— When medications are prescribed for children, follow the doctor's instructions, and always supervise the administration of medicines.

— Clean medicine cabinets and other drug-storage areas regularly, safely disposing of unused or old medicines.

— Keep toxic household products out of the reach of children.

— Be sure not to store medicines and cleaning agents in the same location where foods are stored.

— Don't use lead-base paints on toys, cribs, playpens, and other objects.

DIAGNOSING AND PRESCRIBING FOR MENTAL, SOCIAL, AND EMOTIONAL ILLNESSES

Parents diagnose and prescribe more than just physical health needs. For example, about **113,000 emotionally and socially**

disturbed children are enrolled in special education programs in the United States. The health care needs of many of these children were first detected by parents.

Jack was one such parent. He knew the three main characteristics of children who have good mental and emotional health.

1. They feel good about themselves.
2. They feel good about other people.
3. They are able to cope with problems in their lives.

Jack observed that his 10-year-old daughter Amy did not have these characteristics as she once did. She was depressed, easily angered, and defeated by the simplest problems. Jack spent a great deal of time talking to Amy. From these talks, Jack felt that he at last had determined the cause of his daughter's personality change. His diagnosis was that Amy had been protected too much. She had not been given the opportunities to solve her own problems in life, and she felt helpless and "boxed in." Jack was not sure just how to

Parents prescribe a proper diet, exercise, and rest in order to achieve a normal rate of growth and development for their children.

X-rays, pictures that record the internal condition of the body, help the doctor make a diagnosis.

help Amy. He simply did not have the skills necessary to guide Amy back to good emotional health. For that reason, Jack consulted a child psychologist. The psychologist recommended that Amy be enrolled in a special program for emotionally disturbed children. Do you think that Jack's prescription was the right one?

SPECIALISTS DIAGNOSE AND PRESCRIBE

While parents can often diagnose and prescribe for many of their children's health problems, specialists must be relied upon for solutions to the more serious illnesses.

DIAGNOSING AND PRESCRIBING FOR PHYSICAL ILLNESSES

Measles (rubeola) is a very serious children's disease that is caused by a virus. Measles begins with what at first appears to be a cold or the flu. The child has a high fever, cough, and watery eyes. The doctor watches these symptoms carefully, know-

ing that this could develop into a case of measles. After several days, when tiny white spots appear near the lower molars on the inside of the child's cheeks, the doctor's suspicion increases. When a blotchy red skin rash develops about the child's hairline within the next two days and spreads downward, the doctor can make the diagnosis — measles.

The prescription for measles is bed rest for the child in a somewhat darkened room. Medicine may be given to control the cough. A liquid diet is often prescribed during the period of fever. Family members who have not had measles are told to stay away from the sick child as much as possible during the first four or five days. Measles, at this stage, is contagious (easily caught). The rash comes out fully on the child in two or three days, and then the skin eruptions begin to fade. As the spots disappear, the child improves rapidly. About a week later, the child is usually allowed to play outside with other children, providing all the cold symptoms have disappeared.

Because measles is so serious (leading to pneumonia, ear infections and other illnesses), children should receive a measles **vaccination** at the age of one. With the

The doctor analyzes all information about a patient, makes a diagnosis, and prescribes a treatment.

The pharmacist follows the doctor's directions in filling out prescriptions for medicines and drugs.

vaccination, the doctor may also give a shot of **gamma globulin** (containing natural chemical substances that help fight disease). This prevents the rash and fever the vaccination sometimes produces. Gamma globulin might also be given to young children without vaccinations if they have been near someone who has measles. Gamma globulin can give these children protection against measles for a short time or at least make the disease a little less serious if they do develop this illness.

Mumps is another disease common among children. Pain below and in front of the ear is the first symptom of mumps. Following this, the child may have trouble swallowing and chewing. Finally, the **salivary glands** (which produce moisture in the mouth) located below and in front of the ears may swell and become very tender to the touch. Sometimes only one gland swells or no swelling takes place at all. The child could also develop chills and a fever.

After doctors have diagnosed mumps, they usually prescribe bed rest if the case is severe. Doctors do not want other children near the child with mumps, for the disease can be passed on from about seven (7) days before it appears until a week or 10 days afterwards. When the swelling has gone, the child normally can return to the family and school environment. A vaccination can be given to prevent mumps. It should be given to adolescent boys who have not had mumps since this disease can affect the sex glands. Children with serious diseases should also be given the vaccination. Their body, already weakened by one disease, could not also fight mumps.

DIAGNOSING AND PRESCRIBING FOR EMOTIONAL ILLNESSES

No vaccination is available for **emotional problems.** They can develop at any point in a child's life. Emotional problems, if not diagnosed and treatment prescribed, can cause damage as long lasting as an untreated case of mumps or measles.

Emotional problems can develop within the environment of family, school, or friends or in that private world of the child's mind. Those who can help are psychiatrists (medical doctors specializing in mental and emotional problems) and psychologists (non-medical personnel trained to understand the workings of the human mind).

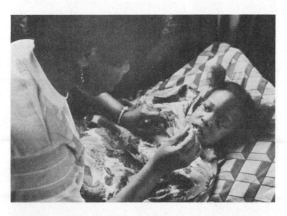

A mother follows the doctor's prescription for her child. It may call for rest in bed, a liquid diet, and some medicine to control coughing.

A child who is extremely aggressive or cruel in his or her behavior toward others may be emotionally ill and in need of special care or rehabilitation.

They work with children to help them find out what is causing their emotional or mental disturbances and learn how to overcome them. Psychiatrists and psychologists may diagnose a child as emotionally or mentally disturbed by observing one or more of the following serious symptoms:

1. **Obsessions** — thoughts that occur so often that they make it difficult for a child to think normally. Some children become obsessed with the idea of dying or being disliked by others.
2. **Compulsions** — desire to repeat certain acts over and over when it is not necessary to do so. A child may have a compulsion to constantly wash the hands, change clothing, or repeatedly lock all the doors in the house.
3. **Extreme aggressiveness** — frequent cruelty to other children or animals. This child always demands to be the leader in games and is unwilling to share with others.
4. **Anxiety** — fear of something unknown or unnamed. The child may feel restless and frightened, but does not know why.

Once specialists have diagnosed children as emotionally disturbed, they may prescribe a number of different treatments or instructional or rehabilitating (rebuilding) actions. The child might be given tranquilizers as a part of the treatment. These are pills containing medicine that produces calmness. The specialist may have the whole family come to meetings where each member's behavior in the home is discussed. If that behavior has in some way helped cause the child's emotional problem, plans are made to change that behavior. This type of communication with the family is an example of an instructional action. A rehabilitation action may take place when the specialist works with the child to help him learn to solve his own emotional problems.

REVIEWING YOUR VOCABULARY

diagnosis	rash
myopia	contagious
prescribe	skin eruptions
ophthalmologist	vaccination
treatment	gamma globulin
instructional-action	mumps
rehabilitating	salivary glands
Poison Control Center	cystic fibrosis
internal medicines	obsessions
accidental poisonings	compulsions
cope	aggressiveness
child psychologist	anxiety
rubeola	tranquilizers
molars	

INCREASING YOUR PERCEPTION

1. List common childhood diseases and identify symptoms of those diseases.
2. Describe the process that parents go through to diagnose children's illnesses.
3. Discuss what illnesses most parents diagnose and prescribe, and discuss which illnesses are likely to prompt parents to take the children to specialists for diagnosis and prescription.
4. Give examples of medical, instructional, or rehabilitating actions that would be directed by the following adults:
   a. Parents
   b. Specialists

Diagnosing and Prescribing Health Care Needs

Parents Diagnosing and Prescribing

– Identifying condition or disease

– Determining the cause or nature of illness

– Selecting a medical, instructional, or rehabilitating action

– Consulting a specialist

Specialists Diagnosing and Prescribing

– Identifying condition or disease

– Determining the cause or nature of illness

– Directing a medical, instructional, or rehabilitating action

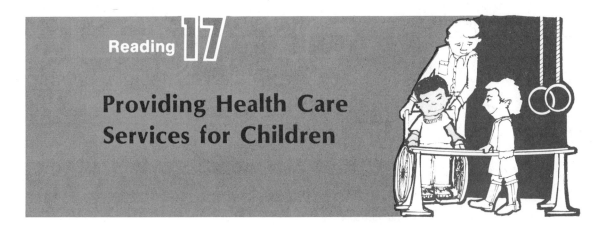

Reading 17

Providing Health Care Services for Children

Through diagnosing, parents and health care specialists identify children's health problems and determine their causes. A treatment, education, or rehabilitation action is then **prescribed.** Adults must follow the prescription to actually provide health care services for children.

Over $60 billion a year is spent on health care in the United States. About 3.5 million people are employed in all health occupations. It is little wonder that children receive better health care today than ever before in the history of the human race.

Children are provided health care services within the **family environment** or in the **hospital and clinic environments.** The service provided could be as simple as that of a parent bandaging a child's cut finger or as complex as that of a hospital rehabilitating a lame child for a period of months. Whether simple or complex, the most important thing is to provide the kind of services children need, when and where they need them.

THE FAMILY HEALTH CARE ENVIRONMENT

Over 6,000 people die from accidental drownings every year in the United States. That didn't mean much to Judy until she saw the limp body of her three-year-old daughter Cathy being lifted from the wading pool by her older sister. "Cathy fell down and was under the water," cried her sister.

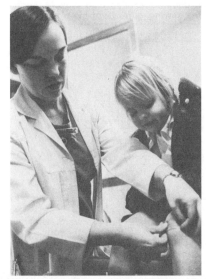

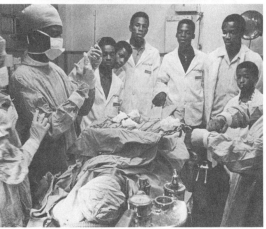

Bandaging a small cut on a child's knee is a form of health care, as is major surgery to save human life.

HOW TO GIVE MOUTH-TO-MOUTH RESUSCITATION

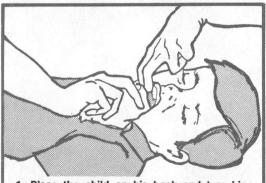

1. Place the child on his back and turn his head to the side. Using your finger or a handkerchief, remove foreign objects, such as food or chewing gum, from his mouth.

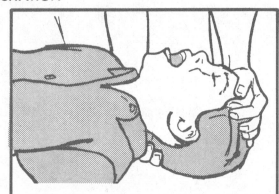

2. Tilt the child's head back so that his chin points upward. His head should be so far back that his neck is arched.

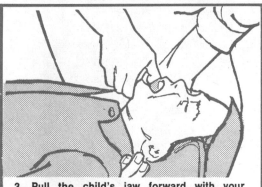

3. Pull the child's jaw forward with your thumb, and hold it there with your fingers. Keep your hand in this position to make sure the mouth stays open.

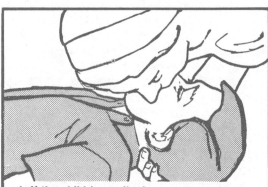

4. If the child is small, place your mouth over both his mouth and nose. Blow into his mouth and nose. Take shallow breaths — about one breath every three seconds.

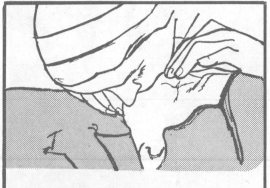

5. If the child is bigger, pinch his nostrils shut, and cover his mouth with your mouth. Blow into his mouth.

6. Remove your mouth and listen for a return rush of air. Then, repeat step 3 (pull the child's jaw forward) and step 4 or 5 (blow into his mouth).

Mouth-to-mouth resuscitation is an important skill for parents as well as others to know if they are to be prepared to protect their children during emergencies.

Judy had left the girls alone for less than a minute. Guilt and fear crowded her mind. Quickly putting those thoughts aside, she automatically began the first aid treatment she had learned years ago. She tilted the child's head back, pointing the chin upward. She moved the lower jaw forward, placed her mouth over Cathy's mouth and nose, and breathed shallow puffs of air into her lungs. Judy counted to three between puffs, creating a breathing rate of about 20 puffs each minute. After a short time, Cathy began coughing. She would live.

FIRST AID TREATMENT

First aid, such as the mouth-to-mouth resuscitation Judy performed on her child, is one form of emergency treatment parents may provide children in the family environment. No matter how well parents protect their children, accidents do happen. A knowledge of some basic first aid skills such as these is very helpful when emergencies in the home arise.

Burns. Cool water should be applied immediately to the skin. This action reduces the pain and keeps swelling at a minimum. Grease must never be applied to a burn. If the burns cause the skin to blister, the child should be taken to the doctor. If the burns are severe enough for hospitalization, the child should be wrapped in a damp sheet for the trip. Often, **sunburn** is treated at home. **Sunburn** can be prevented by keeping children covered with clothing. Products are available that will relieve pain of a mild sunburn. A serious burn of any kind requires a doctor's attention.

Choking on an Object. The child should cough up the object, if possible. If a small child cannot cough up the object, hold the child upside down and pat gently on the back. Never hit the back. If choking is severe, the child should be taken to a doctor or hospital immediately. **Choking can be prevented** by never giving a young child very small toys, little pieces of candy, popcorn, or nuts.

Insect Bites. The bitten area is covered with a damp cloth that has been dipped in baking soda, or cold water and ice can be applied to reduce pain and swelling. Some insects, such as bees, leave stingers in the skin that may be removed with tweezers. If a number of insects have bitten the child, a doctor should be consulted. Many insects have a small amount of venom (poison) in their sting that could make a child seriously ill.

Swallowed Objects. If the swallowed object is blunt, such as a coin, it will probably pass through the child's system during a bowel movement. A child who has swallowed a sharp object, such as a pin or needle, should be taken to a doctor. Such emergencies can be avoided by closing safety pins and by removing dangerous but tempting objects from the child's reach.

PRESCRIBED TREATMENTS

Parents also provide treatment for their children by giving them medicine prescribed by a doctor. The parents must follow the doctor's instructions very carefully, giving the medicine in the proper doses at the hours directed. If directions are not followed properly, the medicine may not be effective. Children have been known to create a fuss about taking medicine, especially if it has

Parents treat their children by giving them medicine according to the doctor's instructions.

a strange taste. This difficulty can often be overcome by mixing the medicine in a little juice, honey, or jelly. Parents must never give children medicine left over from another illness unless the doctor is consulted.

During rehabilitation, a child needs special care and training.

A specialist in the treatment of eye disorders may use special machines to test the vision of children.

REHABILITATION

Parents must provide their children with rehabilitation services in the home from time to time. After an illness or injury, children may require a long recovery period. Parents, following the doctor's instruction, give the child special care, or they help the child perform special exercises that will strengthen the body. For example, a parent whose child had a leg injury could help strengthen leg muscles by massaging them daily. Making sure that the child performed special exercises outlined by the doctor would also help hasten recovery.

Parents whose children develop the eye problem commonly called "lazy eye" must also provide a rehabilitation service. In this condition, one of the child's eyes becomes dominate (stronger) over the other. The child may favor or use the right eye more than the left. In time, the eye used less becomes "lazy." Its muscles become weaker and weaker. To cure this problem, doctors often cover the dominate or stronger eye with a patch. This forces the lazy eye to work. Gradually, the muscles of the lazy eye strengthen, and the condition is improved if the child is willing to wear the eye patch. Parents must make sure that it is worn, because they know that in time the patch will help their child have better eye coordination.

EDUCATION

Education is an important health care service that parents can provide in the home environment. They must teach their children to avoid certain dangers that could be harmful to their health. As children begin to crawl and walk, for example, parents must teach them not to touch a hot stove or stick objects into electrical outlets. Many youngsters become fascinated with fire and must be taught to leave matches alone.

Bottles of medicine, household cleansers, and other containers should be locked up until children can learn to avoid them. Parents can also educate their children about the dangers of playing in abandoned refrigerators and houses.

Wise parents also educate their children about health care specialists outside the home.

Parent: "I am going to the dentist today. You may come with me."

Child: "What's a dentist, Mommy? What do they do?"

Parent: "A dentist takes care of your teeth. You sit in the dentist's special chair that can go up and down. The dentist looks in your mouth with a tiny mirror."

Child: "Will I sit in that chair someday?"

Parent: "Yes. The dentist will become your friend because the dentist will keep your teeth clean and healthy."

If parents teach children that health specialists are their friends, youngsters will not be afraid of them. In fact, many children can be taught to enjoy visiting the office of health care specialists they know.

HOSPITAL AND CLINIC ENVIRONMENTS

While parents can meet many of their children's health care needs at home, they must sometimes depend upon specialists. A child may need an operation or medical treatment that requires technical equipment. Perhaps a rehabilitation program under the guidance of a physical therapist is needed. An educational program in which a child learns to control his or her emotions may be provided by a psychologist.

Health care specialists may provide their services in **hospital and clinic environments.** The hospital is often thought of as a place where people go to get well. Actually, the modern hospital has these four basic functions:

1. Caring for and rehabilitating (restoring) the sick and injured.

Parents must teach children the dangers of such things as abandoned refrigerators or playing with matches. At the same time, they must also remove these hazards from the child's environment.

At a dental clinic, the dentist may educate a child to use the proper procedure for brushing teeth.

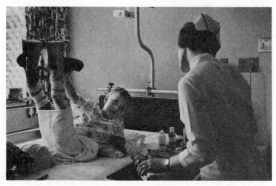

A. Caring for and rehabilitating the sick and injured.

B. Educating hospital personnel and patients.

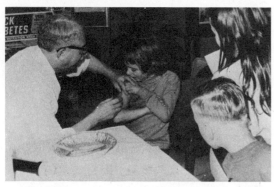

C. Preventing disease through public health programs.

D. Discovering new medical knowledge through research.

The modern hospital has four basic functions.

2. Educating and training doctors, nurses, and other hospital workers, as well as patients who must learn to care for themselves.
3. Preventing disease through public health programs.
4. Discovering new medical knowledge through research.

OWNERSHIP

Who owns the hospitals? Ownership may be classified on either a (1) government (public) or (2) nongovernment (private) basis.

Government hospitals are owned by either federal, state, county, or city governments. These hospitals, whether offering general or special treatment, are responsible to the department or organization of the government that owns it. Money to operate the hospital (operating funds) is provided by that government and often by the patients who use the hospital's service.

Nongovernment hospitals are owned by churches, social organizations, communities, or private corporations. They receive their operating funds from fees paid by patients and gifts from members of the community.

Clinics may be (1) privately owned and operated by one or more doctors, (2) operated by hospitals as an additional service, (3) operated as a community service and housed in a public building, such as a school, or (4) operated as a research center where specialists learn about disease and find cures. All clinics are costly to operate.

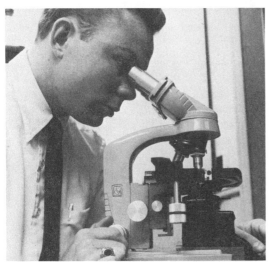

Workers in a research clinic test and observe to discover new knowledge that will be used to provide better services for children.

Privately owned and hospital-based clinics receive their operating funds from fees charged to patients. The community and research clinics are supported through government funds, gifts from private citizens, or money from such organizations as the United Fund.

The medical clinic — whether a privately owned enterprise, community hospital, or research center — is designed for either (1) specific or (2) general treatment. Specific clinics are staffed by doctors who are specialists in one field, such as heart care. General clinics are staffed by specialists from many different fields who can treat a variety of diseases and other illnesses.

SHORT TERM TREATMENT

Treatments offered by hospitals and clinics may be designed to last either a short or long time. Such diseases as chicken pox, appendicitis, or pneumonia usually require rather short treatment, lasting 30 days or less. Just what happens when a hospital staff provides short-term treatment? Following the adventures of a six-year-old girl named Jane during her first visit to the hospital will help you learn what happens.

Jane was playing on a swing when she fell while high in the air. A throbbing pain and swelling in her ankle began. Jane's parents, being very concerned, rushed her to the hospital's emergency ward.

The first person Jane met in the emergency ward was a hospital staff member at the admitting desk. For both legal and medical reasons, Jane's name, address, family doctor's name, nature of injury, and other information were speedily recorded.

A pediatrician, notified by the admitting department that Jane had arrived, came to the emergency ward and examined Jane's ankle. He was assisted by a nurse. Jane liked both of these specialists because their gentleness and smiles greatly relieved her fears. The pediatrician wanted to make sure that the ankle was not broken and ordered an X-ray of her leg. The nurse called an orderly who placed Jane on a bed with wheels and took her to the X-ray department. After the X-ray, Jane was wheeled back to the room.

The doctor quickly received the X-ray. Although it showed that the ankle was only sprained, he decided that Jane should spend the night in the hospital. The fall could have caused internal injuries that might not become evident for a number of hours. A nurse would watch her closely to make sure that no other injuries had occurred. Others whose services helped make Jane's stay pleasant were the dietitian who planned Jane's meal and the workers in the housekeeping department who kept her room clean and neat. In the morning Jane went home. Her ankle was already beginning to heal and her health was improved as a result of the care and attention she had received by members of the hospital staff.

LONG-TERM TREATMENT

Jane's injury was a minor one and her hospital treatment was very short. When

A. Sterilized silverware is placed in plastic bags to keep it germ-free.

B. Containers are sterilized.

C. Nutritious food is prepared for serving to patients.

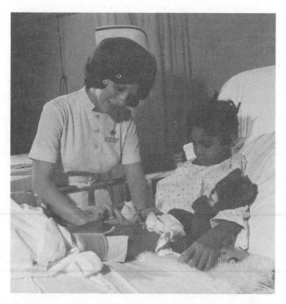

During Jane's stay in the hospital, she received attention and care from the nurse and other workers.

Cleanliness and a proper diet are an important part of hospital care.

children become ill with diseases such as **polio** (that attacks the brain and spinal cord) or **muscular dystrophy** (that affects the muscles), they may spend a very long time in the hospital. Polio, for example, usually requires medicine and physical therapy. Polio weakens muscles which the physical therapist helps the child strengthen through such exercises as swimming and walking in braces. At one time, thousands of children with polio required long-term hospital care. Today, the Salk vaccine has greatly reduced this number. Victims of muscular dystrophy, on the other hand, number over 200,000 in the United States alone. Most of these victims are children. In the common form of the disease, muscles begin to enlarge and deteriorate, eventually ending in the individual's death. Much can be done to help th child throughout the disease. Muscle-stretching exercises and activities that keep the child's body as strong as possible are all a part of long-term hospital care.

One of the most common forms of long-term treatment is **immunization.** The vaccinations (shots) given children in this treatment immunize (protect) them from certain diseases for long periods of time. A community clinic often has a program that provides free vaccinations to neighborhood school children. Below is a list of diseases that can be prevented through vaccinations. Sometimes only one shot is needed. Other diseases require second or third shots called **boosters.**

Wise parents keep an immunization record at home so they will know what vaccinations their children have had and when booster shots are scheduled.

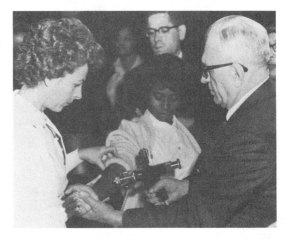

The doctor at this clinic is using a machine called a "Hypospray" that holds enough vaccine to give shots to a large number of children. This is a painless way to give shots since the Hypospray uses air pressure to force the vaccine through pores of the child's skin and into the body.

Disease	Age for First Shot	Number	Boosters
Whooping cough Tetanus Diphtheria	6 weeks to 2 months	3 shots needed, given 1 month apart	at age one, 3, and 6
Polio	6 weeks to 3 months	Taken orally (by mouth) 3 times, 4 to 6 weeks apart	At age 1; again before entering school
Smallpox	15 to 18 months	1 shot	Once every 3 to 5 years or if exposed to smallpox

REHABILITATION SERVICES

Rehabilitation services that rebuild or restore patients to good health are offered by many hospitals. Some clinics specialize in rehabilitation. They have physical therapists on their staff who can help children overcome physical problems resulting from disease or injury. The therapist has been trained through both college and hospital work to treat body defects or weaknesses by exercise, heat, or massage. Children who have injured legs in accidents are helped to walk again by the physical therapist. The therapist may have the child lift a series of increasingly heavier weights with the foot or leg. Taking exercise by swimming or walking with the aid of braces or crutches may be prescribed by the therapist as well as massage.

EDUCATIONAL SERVICES

Hospitals and clinics provide **educational services** not only to children and their parents, but also to health care workers. First of all, children and parents might receive instructions in how to use prescribed medication. Diabetes, for example, is a long-term disease that can be controlled by daily doses of **insulin,** a drug that supplies the correct amount of sugar in the blood. Sometimes insulin can be taken in pill form. In

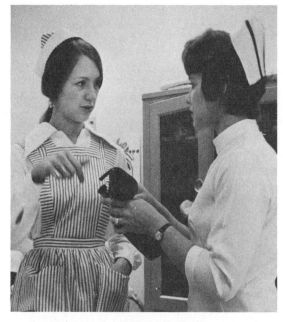

A candy striper must learn how to handle and use certain kinds of medical equipment.

This nurse is instructing a diabetic child in how to take insulin and how to care for the necessary equipment used.

Health care workers are dedicated to the care of their patients.

more serious cases, however, it must be taken as a shot. Hospitals and clinics teach parents or older children how to give a shot and how to care for the necessary medical equipment.

Hospitals and clinics educate many health care workers. Registered nurses (R.N.'s) receive part of their training in hospitals while licensed practical nurses (L.P.N.'s) receive almost all of their training there. Nurse's aides and orderlies are also trained at hospitals and can assist the registered nurse by bathing patients and taking them to other departments for treatment. Many of the personnel that work in the kitchen and laundry of the hospital or clinic also must be trained.

Providing health care, whether in the home or in hospitals and clinics, is an important and often exciting activity. To see the tears disappear on the face of a toddler as her scraped knee is "made all well," or to help save a child's life in the operating room of a hospital offers special rewards beyond words. In the story below, health care workers help a child survive a terrible disease. How does this story make you feel? Does working in a medical atmosphere appeal to you?

Boy Beats Reye's Odds at County

County Hospital physicians beat one-in-five odds against survival in a Reye's Syndrome case Thursday by almost completely exchanging the child's blood with transfusions.

The 2-year-old boy was brought to the hospital in a deep coma. Statistics have shown the death rate in such patients is more than 80 per cent.

Replacement of the blood removed the toxic ammonia that had built up in the system, according to Dr. Willing, acting chief of pediatrics.

Because of a severe lung involvement, the child was completely dependent on artificial respiration for five days.

"The child has made a remarkable recovery and is ready to be discharged," said Dr. Willing.

REVIEWING YOUR VOCABULARY

hospital	physical therapist	dietitian
clinic	specific treatment	polio
drownings	general treatment	muscular dystrophy
first aid treatment	short-term treatment	long-term treatment
venom	emergency ward	diabetes
massaging	pediatrician	R.N.
lazy eye	orderly	L.P.N.
dominate	internal injuries	

INCREASING YOUR PERCEPTION

1. Explain how to administer first aid treatment for burns, choking, and insect bites.
2. Give examples of treatments that may be prescribed by a specialist that would be administered at home by family members.
3. List the names of diseases that require short-term or long-term care.
4. Give examples of diseases that may require rehabilitation or education in order for the children's health to improve.

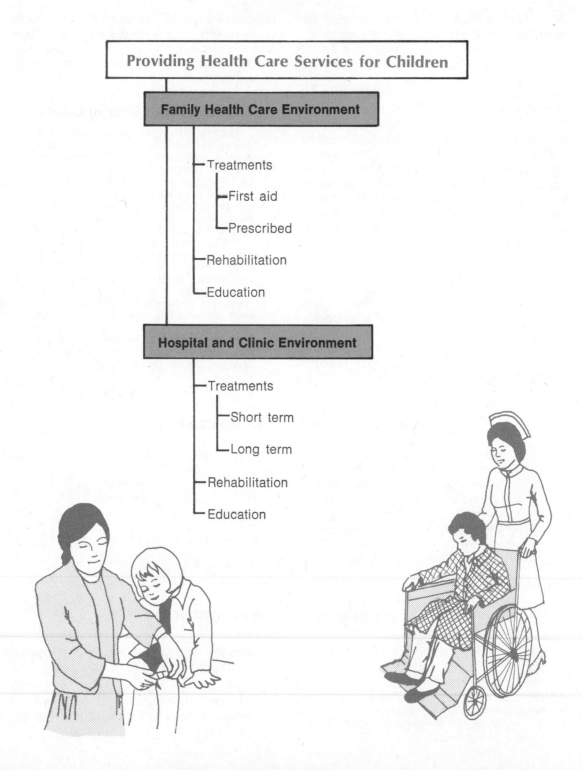

Providing Health Care Services for Children

Family Health Care Environment

├ Treatments
│ ├ First aid
│ └ Prescribed
├ Rehabilitation
└ Education

Hospital and Clinic Environment

├ Treatments
│ ├ Short term
│ └ Long term
├ Rehabilitation
└ Education

Reading 18

Establishing, Researching, and Developing a Child Care Enterprise

Over 69 million children in the United States are under 18 years of age. From the moment of their birth until the day they assume responsibility for themselves, these children must depend upon society to meet their education, protection, and health needs.

About 12 million enterprises are in operation in the United States. A good number of them are helping those 69 million children by producing products or services that teach, protect, or provide health care. Nearly all people have been helped in their development by child care enterprises, and yet enterprises seem to be mysterious operations. How did the enterprise happen to be there when it was needed? How do enterprises begin? How do they know what kind of products to produce? How do enterprises develop these products? This reading answers these questions.

WHAT IS THE PURPOSE?

An enterprise begins when someone decides on a **reason** for it to exist. In other words, an enterprise must have a **purpose** for existing. Deciding on the purpose is a way of saying what the enterprise will be or will not be. For example, around the age of one year, most children are learning to walk and develop coordination. An enterprise may decide that its purpose for existing is to meet children's need to learn to walk properly. The enterprise could produce children's shoes that would both support their

Many products and services are created by enterprises that are established to meet children's needs.

159

feet and allow natural growth. Another enterprise may be established for the purpose of producing toys with different moving parts. This would help children learn how to use their muscles and to develop their ability to grasp. Another enterprise may produce training wheels for bicycles with the purpose of protecting children while they learn to balance the bicycle. Another enterprise may produce medicine to meet children's health needs. Each enterprise is established for **different reasons and purposes.**

If you were to start your own child care enterprise today, what would be its purpose? What children's needs would your enterprise attempt to meet? Perhaps you might decide to produce a toy for toddlers. It could consist of different-size cylinders

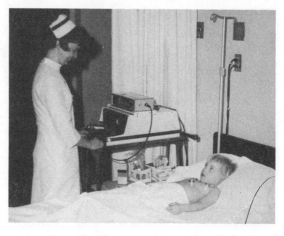

One purpose for establishing an enterprise like a hospital or clinic is to provide children with medical care.

The many enterprises which provide child care products and services form a network of support that can be grouped into three main areas — health, education, and protection.

If you had enough finances you could establish a PROPRIETORSHIP.

When two people share the finances of an enterprise it is called a PARTNERSHIP.

In a CORPORATION, many people buy shares of stock and they own the enterprise as a group.

The kind of private ownership chosen by an enterprise is often determined by finances.

that are stacked inside one another. If you started this type of enterprise, would your purpose be to protect children, to educate children, or to provide for their health care?

WHO IS THE OWNER?

Once the purpose has been decided, the ownership of the enterprise must be determined. The **public** owns some enterprises. This means that all the people in society share in the ownership of these enterprises. Your school, children and family service agencies, and community clinics are some examples of publicly owned enterprises. The operational expenses are usually paid for by taxpayers.

Many enterprises are privately owned. The kind of private ownership chosen by individuals is usually determined by **finance**. A certain amount of finance (money) is needed to begin an enterprise. If you personally had this amount of money yourself or could borrow it from a bank, you might choose **proprietorship** as a form of ownership. Proprietorship means that just **one person owns and operates the enterprise.** The majority of enterprises in the United States (about nine million) are proprietorships. A small nursery school, toy store, or publishing company could be owned by a proprietor.

Perhaps you have half of the amount of money needed to begin an enterprise. You might find a person who would invest the other half. This kind of ownership is called a **partnership**. In a partnership, **two or more people own the enterprise.** There are over 900,000 (nine hundred thousand) partnerships in the United States.

If you only had a small amount of money with which to begin your enterprise, you might decide to form a **corporation**. In a corporation, shares of ownership are sold to the public. People who invest their money in the buying of shares are known as **stockholders**. When people buy shares, they become one of the owners of the corporation. Sears and J. C. Penney are **corporations**

that distribute and sell child care products as part of their business operations.

WHAT IS THE POLICY?

After deciding purpose and ownership, the operators of an enterprise must decide **how and why** they want to provide a product or service. When they have found answers to the how and why, they will have established **policy**. Policy will guide the present and future actions of the enterprise.

This is part of the policy statement of a day care center. It lists what the day care center will do for the children and what the responsibilities of parents are to the school.

POLICIES

1. Hot lunches will be served to full day children. Snacks will be served morning and afternoon to all children.
2. Each child must enter with a medical form and/or a statement from a physician that he or she is free from communicable and infectious disease and is able to participate in a group program. Immunization records must be on file and must be renewed every year or two years according to local regulations.
3. Any medicine to be given a child must be authorized by prescription or written statement of a physician. If a child shows symptoms of illness while in the center, he or she will be

kept isolated from the other children and the parent (or other designated person) will be notified.

4. Parents will provide Happy Time Day Care Center with names of all persons authorized to pick up their children.

5. The Happy Time Day Care Center will be open 12 months a year. The regular week is Monday through Friday. The Center will be closed on New Year's Day, Memorial Day, July the Fourth, Labor Day, Thanksgiving, and Christmas unless otherwise stated in the Center calendar.

The policy statement guides both the enterprise and the parents in providing a service for children.

Enterprises that produce products also form policies. Sometimes policies must be formed because of the **kind** of product the enterprise offers. For example, a manufacturer of infants' play and sleep suits may have a policy of putting each suit through a germ-removing process before packaging them. This policy is very important as it will provide protection of infants' health.

If you were establishing an enterprise that would produce a simple toy, such as a rattle, what kind of policy would you form? Would your policies explain clearly what you would do for the customers? Would your policies be concerned with protecting the health of the infants who would play with the rattle?

ARE PEOPLE AND EQUIPMENT NEEDED?

The enterprise can produce nothing unless it has the **people** and **equipment** necessary to produce a product or provide a service. If an enterprise plans to produce a bathtub for infants, for instance, **researchers** are needed to gather information about infants' bathing needs. The bathtub must not be so shallow that the infant can fall out of

it or so deep that the parent cannot reach in to hold the baby. It must be made of very sturdy material. The research information may then be used in developing a model of the baby's tub. The enterprise might need **engineering technicians** and **drafting people** for this task. **Receiving clerks** make sure the enterprise is supplied with the material needed to make the bathtub. **Machine**

Enterprises use the knowledge and skills of many different workers to produce their products.

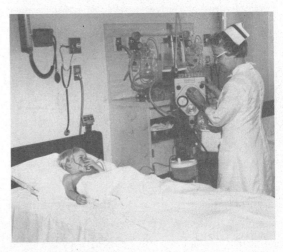

The highly technical equipment used in hospitals and clinics must be operated by skilled workers.

operators and **assembly line workers** actually produce the tub. **Advertising and sales personnel** help inform parents that the tubs for babies have been produced. **Managers** plan, organize, and control the activities of all the **workers**. Many people with different knowledge and skills are needed to produce even the simplest products.

    Equipment must also be carefully selected so that workers can do their best on the job. Some equipment is very simple. If you decided to produce sandboxes, a **hammer, nails,** and a **saw** would complete your equipment needs. However, if the enterprise produced breakfast cereal for children, it might, among other things, need a high-temperature **test oven**. This oven determines the vitamin content of cereals. The right equipment for each process is an important part of a successful enterprise.

RESEARCHING INFORMATION

    If you were starting your own enterprise to manufacture tricycles for children, would you know how large to make the tricycles,

how high to place the seats, or what type of paint would be best for the tricycles? Most enterprises find answers to questions like these through **researching**. By researching, enterprises find answers to how they can meet children's needs in the best possible way. Researching is accomplished in three steps:

- Retrieving Information
- Organizing Information
- Recording Information

    To see how research is done in the real world of work, look over the shoulder of Bob, a research chemist. Bob works for a corporation that produces infant's clothing. He is one of more than 130 thousand chemists employed in the United States, about three-fourths of whom are working for private enterprises. Bob's main job at the corporation is to make sure that the clothing produced will meet the safety standards set by the Flammable Fabrics Act of 1967. The cloth used in the clothing should not burn easily. Bob **retrieves information** by testing the different fabrics to determine their reaction to heat and fire. This research could very easily result in the saving of infant's lives. Bob then **organizes** all his facts and **records**

This technician is operating a special high temperature test oven for use in analyzing the vitamin content of cereal.

Through experimental research, the enterprise can discover new knowledge about how quickly a piece of material used in children's clothing will burn.

the information discovered in the tests. He and other members of the research team **study** this information carefully. If it shows that the material being considered for an infant sleeping suit burns in too short a time, Bob will recommend that some other material be selected for infant's clothing.

Bob performs experimental research. His friend Mary does a different kind of research for another enterprise where she researches the possibility (feasibility) of producing toy telephones. Managers in this company believe that the phones should contain a recorded voice that will actually speak to the child. This will not only help children to improve their speech, but also teach them how to use real telephones.

Mary will begin researching by finding out what age group would use the phone. Her research must also tell the enterprise what size of phone the children could handle and the type of recorded message they would understand and enjoy. She will retrieve information about children by **reading** from books stored in the library and by **interviewing** experts in child growth and behavior. She learns that the toy telephone would be best suited for children about 18 months old. She also learns that these children are not able to use their hands to pick up small objects, so the telephone should have large parts. She learns that children understand best those sentences that are short and simple.

Mary **organizes** her information according to such topics as age, speech development, and size of product. She then records the information by typing it in the form of a report.

From research information such as Mary's, the enterprise managers must decide whether it is feasible (possible or likely) to produce a product or service that will meet children's needs. After looking at the research information, the enterprise operators may decide to produce the item. Or

Historical research is the gathering, sorting, and classifying of information already existing in books and other publications so that it can be used in developing new products and services.

Enterprises use research surveys to gather information about consumer needs.

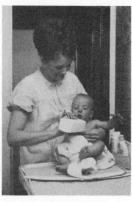

A mother does her own research so she can select goods and services that will meet the needs of her children.

The design for this kit began as an idea to show children how well they were brushing their teeth.

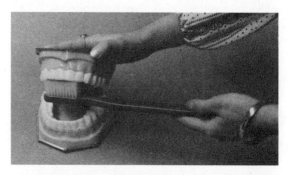

Designers prepare models from rough sketches to illustrate the actual size and shape of the finished product before it is produced in large quantities.

they may decide that it is not possible to produce the product because of the expense involved, or lack of necessary materials or knowledge.

If you were planning to operate your own enterprise, you would also research. If you wanted to make a little wooden step stool to enable toddlers to reach the bathroom sink, researching would tell you the average weight and height of toddlers. You could use that information in deciding how big to make the wooden step stool.

Just how important is research? There are over 5,400 industrial research laboratories in existence. Enterprises spend more than 12 million dollars each year on research projects. Research is very important!

DEVELOPING IN A CHILD CARE ENTERPRISE

Most children begin brushing their teeth when about two years old. Rather, that is when they **should** begin brushing. However, standing in front of a mirror pushing a brush up and down against their teeth may not seem like fun, so many children find a variety of ways to escape this routine. Most children simply do not understand the importance of brushing. It is difficult for them

to realize that their teeth become dirty with decaying food just as their hands and faces may become dirty. However, enterprises have developed products that help children learn good dental care in enjoyable ways.

This kit began as a designer's **idea**. The designer wanted to find a way to show children how much plaque (decaying food) was on their teeth before brushing. This could be done, the designer thought, by providing children with harmless tablets that, when chewed, would stain the plaque on their teeth a bright red. These tablets would be part of a toothsaver kit. The designer also decided that children needed to learn how to properly brush their teeth. A big model of teeth and a giant toothbrush would

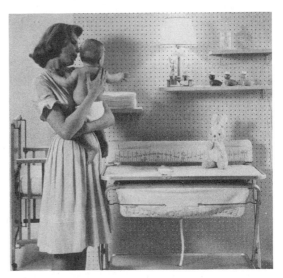

Child care products are tested by people who would be most likely to buy and use them.

The designer goes through these steps to develop a product:
- Thinking of an idea
- Researching
- Drawing a sketch
- Making a model
- Testing

be perfect tools with which to show children how to care for their teeth.

The designer drew **rough sketches** of the kit and teeth on paper. A number of sketches were made before the designer was satisfied. Next, the designer made **clay models** of the kit, teeth, and brush. Because the designer did not like the big brush, a few changes were made in the design. Afterwards, the designer felt that the time for **testing** had arrived.

A panel discussion allows the enterprise to discover what consumers like or dislike about the product or service being developed.

TESTING A PRODUCT OR SERVICE

Testing is often done through a consumer survey. Consumers are people who will buy the product. Finding out what they think about the design of a product can be very valuable to the enterprise. Consumer surveys are conducted by specialists who know how to get useful information from consumers, compile the information, and decide how it affects the design itself.

Suppose that the new children's toothbrush kit, teeth, and brush are being surveyed. The survey team only wants to interview children and their parents. When the child and parent have been selected, they are shown the designer's models. After examining them, the children and their parents

Top management is responsible for approving each stage of design development.

developing. The establishing activity is repeated every time a new enterprise is formed, no matter how large or small it may be. Almost every product or service that is on the market today began with researching and developing activity. These work activities help an enterprise develop products and services that meet children's needs for health, education, and protection.

REVIEWING YOUR VOCABULARY

coordination
grasp
training wheels
cylinders
ownership
operational
  expenses
finance
proprietorship
partnership
corporation
share
stockholders
policy
manufacturer
engineering
  technicians
drafting people
receiving clerks
machine operators

assembly line operators
test ovens
vitamin content
retrieving
organizing
recording
chemists
safety standards
Flammable Fabrics Act
interviewing
feasible
operators
plaque
rough sketches
clay models
consumer survey
compile
panel
preference

are asked their opinions. The children might even be allowed to actually use the kit or brush.

The enterprise might also hold a panel discussion to find out **why** the children liked or disliked the kit, teeth, and brush. The panel could include 10 toddlers. Each child would be led in discussion by a research worker. The statements of each child are recorded. The research team might hold 10 or more such panels.

At the end of the survey, all the recorded information is organized and studied. Management may direct the designers to change the product in some way. The final design is returned to management for approval. The reason one design is chosen over another may be because research showed that consumers liked that design best.

Usually a number of meetings take place between designers and management as the product or service is developed. The design must meet both enterprise and consumer needs and both needs are considered in each meeting. At last, final approval is given and an idea has become a real product or service.

All enterprises follow the basic work activities of establishing, researching, and

INCREASING YOUR PERCEPTION

1. Identify the purposes of three local enterprises.
2. Discuss the type of ownership you would probably find in an elementary school, a hospital, or a toy factory.
3. Identify the rules and regulations that must be checked when a family or an enterprise is established.
4. Explain how research is used by the enterprise to determine what goods should be provided for children.
5. Identify research methods used by you and your parents to gather information about a child care good or service.

6. Describe the research method you would use to gather more information about working with children.

7. Explain the processes or steps that are followed in developing a good such as a baby bottle.

8. Explain the processes or steps that are followed in developing a service such as a nursery school.

9. Identify methods that may be used to test goods and services.

10. Explain why management approval is necessary during the development of a good or service.

11. List and describe examples of how you have used the developing process in your personal life.

Establishing, Researching, and Developing a Child Care Enterprise

Establishing a Child Care Enterprise

- Determining purpose and deciding ownership
- Establishing policy
- Identifying needed people and equipment

Researching Information for Child Care

- Gathering information
  - Retrieving information
  - Organizing and recording information
- Determining feasibility of starting the enterprise

Developing a Child Care Enterprise

- Developing an idea for the enterprise
- Making a sketch or outline
- Making and testing the service
- Obtaining management approval

Reading 19

Selecting Personnel and Providing Child Care Services

Mary has helped thousands of parents meet their infant's health needs. Mary is not a doctor or nurse as you might think, nor is she a social worker for a children and family service agency. Mary operates a machine that fills glass jars with nutritious baby food. Her employer depends upon Mary to play her important part in providing babies with the food they need to grow strong and healthy.

Mary is one of about 83 million people who work for enterprises in the United States. Enterprises select these workers as carefully as possible. Without them, enterprises simply would not be able to function. No products would be produced. No services would be provided. For those reasons, enterprises spend more money hiring, training, and employing workers, such as Mary, than on any other activity.

Producing products and providing services require the knowledge and skills of many different workers.

Enterprises need workers, but workers need enterprises, too. Enterprises provide an opportunity for people to make a living by using their knowledge and skills. In other words, enterprises and workers depend upon one another. Neither can accomplish much alone. Working together as a team, they can produce the products or provide the services that make life so much better for everyone.

GATHERING PEOPLE RESOURCES

Ruth Larsen's enterprise was not a large corporation. In fact, Ruth was the **entire enterprise.** She produced Christmas stockings for children. The stockings had become very popular products in her city. Each year, more and more parents ordered them for their children. Finally, more orders were coming in than Ruth could fill alone. She needed **help**.

Ruth's problem was really no different than the problems experienced by large corporations. Both need the resource of people who can perform the **work** necessary for production. Ruth's work was rather simple. To produce her product, she first cut out a long stocking from red felt. She then cut out a Christmas tree design from green felt. She glued the design on one piece of the stocking and then sewed both pieces together. A "Ruth Original Christmas Stocking" was created!

The time it took Ruth to produce the stockings was a problem. She wasn't par-

ticularly fast with needle and thread. For that reason, she decided she would hire someone to sew the stockings together while she cut and glued. The person would have to be skilled in sewing and really enjoy it, for Ruth planned to produce stockings until close to Christmas time.

Although Ruth did not know it, her future employee was a grandmother of four who lived on the other side of the city. Mrs. Roberts loved to sew and was very good at it. As the Christmas season drew near, Mrs. Roberts wished there was some way she could use her talent to earn a little extra money for Christmas gifts. She needed work such as Ruth's enterprise offered. Ruth needed Mrs. Roberts talents. Now all that was necessary was for Ruth to meet Mrs. Roberts.

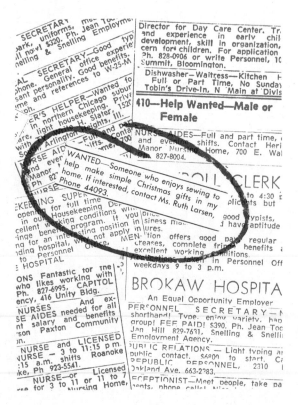

Enterprises can recruit personnel by placing ads in the Help Wanted section of a newspaper.

RECRUITING

Recruiting is the way in which enterprises and workers find each other. Ruth decided to recruit someone skilled in sewing in about the same ways as larger enterprises recruit their people resources. Ruth advertised the sewing job in the **Help Wanted** section of the local newspaper.

> Wanted — Someone who enjoys sewing to help make simple Christmas gifts in my home. If interested, contact Ms. Ruth Larsen, phone 44093.

Ruth could have listed the job with the state employment office or advertised over the local radio station. She might have also used the most common recruiting method of all — by "word of mouth." This simply means that a number of people pass along the word that an enterprise needs a particular kind of worker. In your own school, you might use a bulletin board or circulate a written message to let others know about a job opening.

APPLYING

Many people often apply for one certain job. They may also apply at a number of enterprises. This means that both enterprise and worker must **select**. The enterprise selects the worker who seems best qualified for the job. The worker selects the job that has the most appeal for him or her. Mrs. Roberts, after reading about the sewing job in the newspaper, took samples of her sewing and went to see Ruth. Mrs. Roberts and her sewing ability impressed Ruth, and so she was hired. In larger enterprises, selecting an employee is a little more complex.

Jane, for example, wanted a summer job. She was 15 years old and felt that it was time she earned her own spending money and learned a little about the world of work. Being interested in manufacturing, she decided that the best way to learn more about it was to work in a manufacturing plant. Jane knew of a large plant that produced swing sets for children near her home.

Before Jane could actually apply for a job in the plant, she had to visit the local Social Security office and ask for a Social Security number. Almost all enterprises will only hire workers with Social Security numbers. This number is required by the govern-

Both public and private employment agencies maintain lists of available jobs and people who are seeking work.

Almost all workers need a Social Security card. Workers 16 years of age or younger may need to obtain a work permit.

ment in order to keep a record of a worker's retirement funds. Because Jane is under 16 years of age, she must also get a work permit at her school. Work permits are required by law as a means of protecting young workers.

When Jane arrived at the manufacturing plant, she was first given an application form to fill out. This form provides the enterprise with such information about an employee as:

Name
Address
Telephone number
Social Security number
Record of past working experience
Outside interests (such as hobbies)
References (names of people other than relatives who will recommend the applicant)

Under the Civil Rights Act, the person applying for a job does **not** have to supply the enterprise with such information as age (unless under 16), race, or religion. In this way, a person will be considered or rejected for a job only on the basis of ability — not age, color of skin, or religious belief.

INTERVIEWING

By filling out the application form, Jane was able to tell the enterprise what she **could** do as a worker. The employer interviewed Jane personally to find out whether she **will** do what she says she can do. Jane, like other applicants, used the interview as a means of learning more about the enterprise and the job being offered.

During the interview, the employer asks questions. Replies by the applicant will help determine whether he or she is the kind of worker who will remain on the job for a long period of time and will get along well with others. Answers to questions will also reveal whether the applicant likes to accomplish a great deal, is realistic, and will stick to a task until it is completed.

Jane also asked questions as she was being interviewed. She wanted to know

Applying for a job begins with filling out an application for employment.

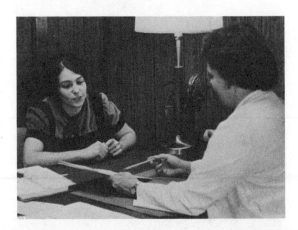

During the interview, the employer may ask specific questions about answers given on the application blank. She may also test the applicant with questions that will reveal the applicant's knowledge of the work she will be performing.

whether the job would really help her in deciding upon a career. Would the job help her test her abilities and skills in her field of interest? If she found she really liked working in the plant, could the job serve as a stepping stone to more responsible work.

When the interview ended, Jane was given a test that measured her skills and abilities in operating a simple machine. During this time, the employer checked the information Jane supplied on the application form. Jane was honest in presenting information about herself. Some applicants might not be.

HIRING

As it happens in many cases, several people were qualified for the job that Jane wanted. The employer thought about each **person** carefully. Jane was chosen over the others for one important reason. She showed a real eagerness to accept the challenges of the job. When offered the position, Jane **accepted**. She felt that the job would help her learn more about manufacturing, and it would help her decide whether this was

the kind of work she wanted to do in the future.

Jane was enrolled in a short training program. She learned how to operate a piece of machinery safely and effectively. If Jane does her work well, she may be promoted to a better job and higher pay. If she fails at her job, she may be **fired** (removed from the employment of the enterprise). It is up to Jane to do her job well if she wishes to be recognized as a good worker.

OTHER RESOURCES

People are the most important resource an enterprise has. Enterprises also need other resources to produce products or provide services. First, they need **knowledge**. Knowledge helps people to understand the product or service being produced, the consumers who will use the product or service, and the enterprise's own ability to actually produce.

Another resource enterprises must have is **finance**. Finance is money. Money that an enterprise may use in producing a product is called **capital**. Some capital is **working**

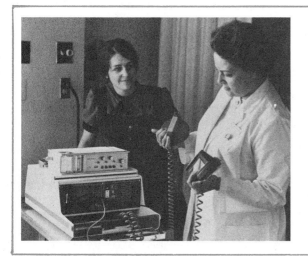

In many enterprises, new employees must become skillful in the operation of specialized machinery.

PEOPLE

KNOWLEDGE

FINANCE

INDUSTRIAL RESOURCES

UTILITIES

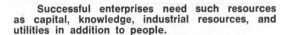

Successful enterprises need such resources as capital, knowledge, industrial resources, and utilities in addition to people.

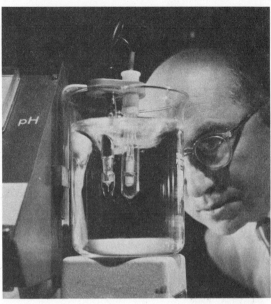

The research analyst brings exact knowledge to the enterprise and helps it develop a product or service that meets child care needs.

Most products are made from a variety of materials. **Legos®**, for example, are **plastic** blocks with wheels, gears, and other simple items. Children can make clocks, houses, and even bridges from Legos. For an enterprise to produce a product like this, **industrial resources**, such as plastic and metal, must be gathered. An enterprise can either **make** an industrial resource or **buy** it from another company. If you and your friends decided to produce phonograph records that would help toddlers learn the alphabet, would you buy the recording equipment, rent it, or make it yourself?

Light, heat, power, and sanitation are all utility resources that every enterprise depends upon. How could a modern enterprise exist without such **utility services** as telephones, electricity, water, sewage service, or fuel? Public and private industries produce and provide these utility services to enterprises.

for the enterprise as it is used to buy material and to hire employees. It is known as **working capital**. Some capital is **fixed** in the investment of tools, equipment, and buildings, and is known as **fixed capital**.

Enterprises depend upon utility services such as light, heat, power, and sanitation.

4. NECKLINE FINISH
COLLAR

Pin interfacing to WRONG SIDE of collar. Cut outer corners diagonally to 1/4" INSIDE seam line. Baste.

Stitch facing to collar along UN-NOTCHED edges, RIGHT SIDES TOGETHER.

To reduce bulk, GRADE SEAM ALLOWANCES: Cut seam allowances to graduated widths. Cut interfacing close to stitching. Cut stitched corners diagonally.

Turn RIGHT SIDE OUT. Press.

Pin collar to neck edge, RIGHT SIDES UP, matching notches, circles to shoulder darts, and back edges. Baste, stretching collar to fit.

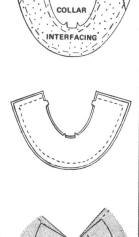

Working drawings are similar to the assembly instructions prepared for model kits and dress patterns.

PREPARING THE PLAN OF ACTION

Harry was very proud of his new factory. It contained the best machinery money could buy. He had hired a fine staff of workers. Working as a team, the employees would produce long, plastic tunnels that Harry himself had designed. Children playing in these tunnels would develop their large muscles and coordination. A few imaginations would be sparked, too! In a child's mind, the tunnel could become a dark cave or a rocket to the moon. When children were finished playing, parents could fold the tunnel up and store it away. Harry was confident his product would be very successful!

When the first tunnel rolled off the production line, Harry's confidence suffered a terrible blow. The tunnel looked more like a large plastic ring than a tunnel. It would not unfold.

What did Harry do wrong? Examination showed that Harry did not prepare a plan of action before he produced the product.

Harry's plan should have described his product through **drawings** and **working models**. It should have **specified** (stated exactly) what materials and supplies, equipment, people, and **process** would be necessary to produce his tunnels.

The drawings would have shown Harry each **individual part** of his product and how they would look when assembled. From these drawings, an engineer or draftsman could have made an actual **working model** of the tunnel. The model might have been **tested** at a nursery school or kindergarten. During the test, children might have found problems with the tunnel that could have been **corrected** before production. One of the problems with Harry's tunnel was that it would not unfold easily. Once unfolded, its sides tore with little effort. Harry needed to use thicker plastic. If Harry would only have made and tested a model of his product, he would certainly have been more successful.

After the tunnel was tested, the plan would have guided Harry in specifying the kind of equipment and workers he would need before going into production. The process used in producing could have been specified, too.

SPECIFYING IS IDENTIFYING:

MATERIALS, SUPPLIES AND EQUIPMENT   PEOPLE   PROCESSES

Enterprises must be careful not to make the same mistake that Harry made. Before producing a product, they must plan the product and the items needed to produce the product. They must make and test a model of the product. Planning takes time. **Not** planning wastes both time and money.

PRODUCING PRODUCTS AND PROVIDING SERVICES

A product or service is produced after a particular process for production is selected. Ruth had her favorite process for producing Christmas stockings. The plant that hired Jane had its own way of producing a product. Poor Harry's chosen process didn't work at all because he neglected to plan in the beginning. Successful enterprises carefully select production methods or processes that will meet all of their requirements.

SELECTING A PRODUCTION METHOD

An enterprise selects a method after considering these elements:

1. The availability of **equipment**.
2. The **ability to produce**.
3. The standards of **quality** that the enterprise must achieve.
4. The availability of **workers**.
5. The **ability to move** materials during production.
6. The **cost** of producing.

After the management of the enterprise approves a particular production method, the necessary equipment, supplies, and materials are brought into the enterprise. Then production may actually begin. Here is how Ruth produces her Christmas stockings product.

PRODUCING A PRODUCT

The production process actually begins with raw materials that will eventually be used for the product. The felt for Ruth's stockings began as the raw material of wool. Wool like other raw materials — such as wood, grain, and ore — come from nature. These materials must first be **refined** (improved). This may be by cutting the material,

This pacemaker, used to regulate the beat of the human heart, will be tested in the laboratory many times before it is used by medical specialists to save lives.

The production begins by carefully examining plans and considering six factors.

Designers and engineers confer with management during the development of new ideas for products and services.

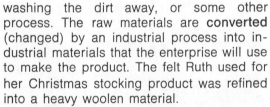

A farmer cultivates cotton plants which produce the raw materials that will be used to make children's clothing.

washing the dirt away, or some other process. The raw materials are **converted** (changed) by an industrial process into industrial materials that the enterprise will use to make the product. The felt Ruth used for her Christmas stocking product was refined into a heavy woolen material.

The industrial materials are usually made into parts. Ruth uses a pattern to cut stocking parts from strips of felt. She cuts the design of a Christmas tree or star from another piece of felt. She glues the design on the front part of the felt stocking. The front and back parts are then assembled by the sewing process. The Christmas stockings, like all child care products begin as raw material, are changed into industrial material, made into parts, and then assembled as they move through several work stations in an assembly line.

PROVIDING A SERVICE

A service enterprise, such as a clinic, begins its programs with raw materials, too. These raw materials are in the form of rough ideas that are discussed and changed until the service to be provided begins to take shape. These ideas are converted into a rough outline of the service.

A service like a manufactured product, is composed of a combination of smaller parts. The approved outline of the service contains the details of these parts. Each detail must fit the overall plan for the service. If a detail does not fit, it is changed and improved.

A clinic uses a different type of assembly line when children receive their inoculations against disease. It uses products and the skills of certain people to provide a service. All the parts to provide the service are made ready. A nurse fills a syringe with vaccine. The doctor wipes the child's arm with alcohol to remove germs and then injects the vaccine. Another nurse places a bandage on the child's arm. With children

This cereal product is prepared for distribution by packaging, inventorying, and shipping.

For: September 23, 1973

I. Statement of Purpose
   By having the book Crow Boy read to them, the children should become aware that there are people in other places who live differently than they do. In the character of Chibi they will see a young Japanese boy going to school in a much different manner than they do. The book also points out that a person should not be judged rashly. This is implied in the story. I do not expect all the children to grasp this idea, but I think many will.

II. Statement of Procedures
   A. Begin by telling the children the name of the book and then saying that Crow Boy is a rather unusual name. Ask them if they know anyone named Crow Boy. Then tell them that Crow Boy didn't live in a city like Peoria, but that he lived in another country very, very far away. Tell them to listen to the story and then we can find out why Crow Boy had such an unusual name.
   B. Read the story to them. Hold book open while reading so they can follow the pictures.
   C. Ask them if they think that Crow Boy's school was like theirs. Have them name a few of the differences. If no one responds mention how the school looked very different, the children dressed differently and wrote differently. Then ask why he was called Crow Boy.

III. Materials to be
   Crow Boy by Taro

IV. Method of Evalua
   Watch the pupils   f the book
   is holding their   llowing
   the reading.

V. Summary of the L
   At the conclusio   e the
   same way and tha   e do.

The teacher's daily lesson plan is a way of preparing to provide the service of education.

moving through the assembly line, the clinic provides the inoculation service.

PREPARING FOR DISTRIBUTION

Both a product and a service must be prepared for distribution. Distribution is the process that brings the product or service to consumers.

Before a product can be sent to consumers, it must be packaged, labeled, and stored. The product may be packaged in a strong box that offers protection against damage by rough handling or dampness. The box is labeled so that the product inside is identified for consumers. These boxes are then put in crates. Inventory is taken (products are recorded) and the boxes stored until shipment to consumers. Storage is usually in a warehouse. From the warehouse, the boxes are loaded onto trucks or trains and sent where they are needed.

Child care services are also distributed to consumers. A mobile (traveling) clinic, for instance, distributes medical help to many people as it moves into different locations to provide the service. Police may provide a service to children in a community by visiting schools or youth clubs to promote bicycle safety on the streets.

WORKING TOGETHER

Enterprises can produce products and provide services only because many people know how to do their jobs and are willing to work together. Workers, under the direction of management, have gathered resources, prepared a production plan, and produced and distributed products. This process is repeated every day so that enterprises can manufacture and provide health, education, and protection products and services for children. Now that you know the production process, does manufacturing a child care product or providing a service for children appeal to you?

REVIEWING YOUR VOCABULARY

nutritious	knowledge
hiring	finance
training	capital
employing	working capital
production	industrial resources
recruiting	utility services
advertised	plan of action
word of mouth	working model
circulate	producing
qualified	raw materials
social security	refined
retirement	converted
work permit	industrial process
application form	assembled
references	syringe
Civil Rights Act	vaccine
accomplish	injects
realistic	distribution
abilities	packaged
skills	labeled
enrolled	stored
effectively	warehouse

INCREASING YOUR PERCEPTION

1. Develop questions which employers could ask during an interview that would tell them about the applicant's personality.
2. Identify places where you could look to find information about available part time jobs.
3. Identify skills and abilities (job specification) needed by a parent to operate a home successfully.
4. Identify skills and abilities (job specification) needed by child care workers, such as teacher's aides, to be successful in their job.
5. Identify the resources that must be gathered by the enterprise to prepare to provide a day care service.
6. Describe how working drawings are developed for a product such as a baby bottle, or a service such as the nursery school.
7. Identify ways to test a working model of a product such as a baby bottle or a service such as a nursery school.
8. Specify the people, materials and supplies, equipment and processes you would use when preparing to provide the service of babysitting.
9. Gather resources, make and test a plan of action to prepare for a personal goal.
10. Identify the production processes your home economics class would use if asked to produce 35 dish towels for the kitchen.
11. Identify the production processes your home economics class would use in providing a nursery school for young children.
12. Explain how you might use the inventory skill in your personal life.

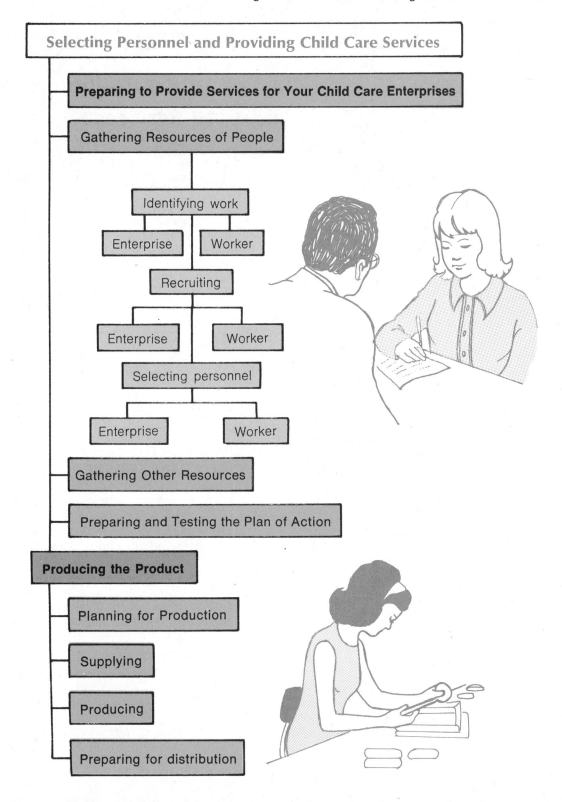

Selecting Personnel and Providing Child Care Services

Preparing to Provide Services for Your Child Care Enterprises

Gathering Resources of People

Identifying work

Enterprise / Worker

Recruiting

Enterprise / Worker

Selecting personnel

Enterprise / Worker

Gathering Other Resources

Preparing and Testing the Plan of Action

Producing the Product

Planning for Production

Supplying

Producing

Preparing for distribution

Selling and Controlling Child Care Services

What does the word **selling** mean to you? Perhaps you think of a salesperson in the children's department of a large store, explaining why one brand of clothing may serve a purpose better than another. Or you may think of the salesperson who represents the manufacturer and sells the clothing to the department store directly from the manufacturer. These are both examples of selling. Selling, however, involves more than just these two kinds of activity.

Would the picture and caption below make you want to buy the product if you were a parent? Publicity Release —

THE GOOD THINGS IN LIFE for baby include a selection of Pampers. A "pampered" junior looks over the different sizes made just for him: Newborn, in quantities of 30, for babies up to 11 pounds; Daytime, in packages of 15 and 30, for babies over 11 pounds; and Overnight, extra absorbent for babies over 11 pounds whenever added absorbency is needed, such as nighttime, trips, and naps.

Selling means **telling** consumers that a product or service is ready for their use. Selling also **explains** how the product or service will meet consumers' needs and therefore be valuable to them. When consumers buy a child care product, the enterprise receives money it needs to pay for the cost of production and other expenses. The money that an enterprise spends on production and receives through selling products must be **controlled** very carefully. Between 9,000 and 10,000 new enterprises fail each year because poor control of their business resulted in their not making a profit.

PROMOTING THE CHILD CARE SERVICE

Many enterprises employ a **promotion manager** or hire a specialist whose job it is to create a **plan** that will **inform** consumers about products and influence consumers to buy them.

A promotion plan may involve both advertising and publicity. The plan could be designed to last six months or a year. Throughout this period, the promotion manager or specialist must see that each part of the plan is carried out.

ADVERTISING

This newspaper advertisement is telling parents what kind of clothing they can buy for their children and where it is available.

Kids'll be sporting it back-to-class in easy-living gear. Things like knit pants, tops, suits, and zip-on sweater dresses. We have 'em and more!

Quincy's

Many enterprises hire the services of professional advertising agencies to publicize and promote their products and services.

The advertisement also influences parents to buy the clothing by pointing out some of its desirable qualities. The same clothing could be advertised on radio and television. Telling the consumers about the product in different ways is part of a promotion plan.

It costs money for an enterprise to advertise its products. Newspapers sell space in their pages. Radio and television sell broadcast time. To make sure that their advertisements are worth the money spent on them, many enterprises buy the services of an advertising agency. The agency is expert in knowing how to reach consumers and influence them to buy a certain product.

It will select the right method of advertising. It will also research the consumer market, write the advertisement, and design it for the enterprise.

Suppose an enterprise has just created a product that will end the tiresome business of having to sterilize baby bottles. This product is a pre-sterilized liner for the bottle. When baby has finished with the meal, the liner is simply thrown away. This is convenient for the mother. The liner assures her that baby will always have sanitary food. Using it makes it easier for her to feed **her** baby.

The agency creating the advertisement for these liners for baby bottles first decides that its **objective** is to **inform** parents about the liner. The agency's **goal** is to **influence** a certain number of parents to respond to the advertisement by buying the liners.

To influence a consumer to buy demands a **communication** between enterprise and consumer. For this reason, the agency chooses a **communication objective**. The objective in creating an advertisement is to have parents think when they see it, "Those liners would certainly save a lot of time and work, and they are safe, too!" The agency states a communication goal of how many parents the advertisement should reach. It may decide that 30 or 40 percent of the parents in the community should see the advertisement.

Even the package is designed to attract the attention of potential buyers.

The advertiser may choose to run the advertisements in a journal or periodical magazine which is intended to report new knowledge to parents and child care specialists.

SELECTING A MEDIA

What kind of parents would want the bottle liners? The agency identifies them by their age, educational background, location, and interest. Parents who would be interested in these liners are identified as in the 20 to 30 age group, have at least completed high school, live in the local community, and want to care for their infants in the safest way possible. Then the agency decides what kind of **media** would best inform these parents. It might be a visual media, such as newspapers or magazines; audio media, (such as radio, telephone); or audiovisual media, such as television.

The agency decides to advertise the baby bottle liners in a magazine for new parents. In this way, the advertisement is sure to reach the group of consumers for which it is intended. Television and radio advertisements would be seen and heard by more people, but many of them would not be parents who would want the bottle liners. Using a magazine as the media, the agency chooses the form of advertisement — in this case, words and illustration.

If you were a parent, would this magazine advertisement influence you to buy the baby bottle liners?

USING PUBLICITY TO PROMOTE THE SERVICE

Another way of promoting a product is by **publicity**. Publicity is a form of advertising at **no cost** to the enterprise. The objective in getting publicity is for an enterprise to present a product in such an interesting way that radio, television, or newspapers will tell about it free of charge because it is interesting or newsworthy.

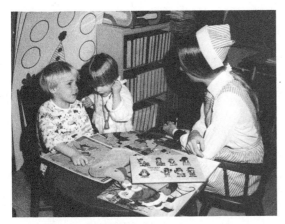

An educational puzzle that helps children understand hospitals better could receive news coverage as a publicity item.

In one form of direct sales, the enterprise sends a representative to demonstrate the use of the products or services being offered.

Suppose a publishing company wants publicity for a new children's book it has just produced. The book, **Bear Learns to Count**, is designed to help toddlers learn the meaning of numbers. How could this book have publicity value? Many such books are on the market. **Bear Learns to Count**, however, does receive quite a bit of publicity on television and in the newspapers for a very good reason. It was written by an 80-year-old woman just beginning a new career as a writer of children's books.

Enterprises may also receive publicity when they inform television stations or other media of events that might be of interest to people in the community. Suppose an enterprise produced a special game called "Get Well Soon." It is designed to help children understand how hospitals take care of them. The game might be part of the hospital's new program to help children overcome their fear of hospitals. If the program is successful, a newspaper might send a reporter to the hospital to take photographs and interview children who have used the game. A photograph such as this might then appear in the newspaper with a story. Enterprises also send photographs of new products to newspapers and magazines in hopes of receiving publicity.

SELLING

Once consumers have been informed about a child care product through advertising or publicity, the product is made available to them through **direct** or **indirect** selling. In direct selling, there is personal contact between the enterprise and the consumer. The publisher of **Bear Learns to Count** might have salespeople sell the book directly to libraries or schools. You may have participated in direct selling by selling candy or candles for a school club or organization.

Indirect selling involves little or no personal contact between the enterprise and consumer. The producer of swings and other playground equipment could sell these products either (1) to **retailers** who then sell the products directly to consumers or (2) to **wholesalers** who purchase large amounts of the products and then sell smaller amounts to retailers. Most parents buy their children's food, toys, and other products from retailers who operate stores.

If you were operating your own child care enterprise, what type of promotion would you choose? If you wanted to advertise your product or service to a large number of people in the community, would you buy space in a newspaper? Could you find something interesting about your product so that you could get free publicity on radio or television? When selling your product, would you most likely use the direct method? If other students were willing to act as wholesalers or retailers, would indirect selling be best for you?

After consumers buy a product, how does an enterprise bring the product to consumers? Getting products to consumers is called **distributing** and there are four different ways of making distribution.

DISTRIBUTION CHANNELS

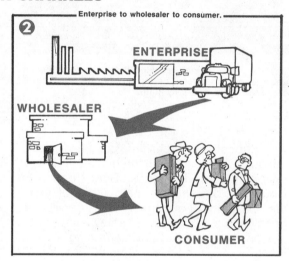

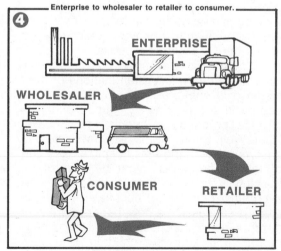

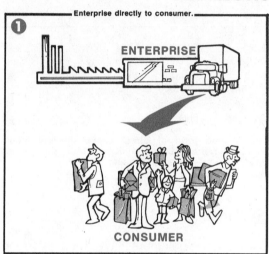

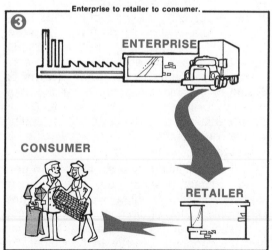

There are four basic ways for the enterprise to get its product or service to consumers. Each way is a channel of distribution. The channel selected is decided by the distance between the enterprise and consumer, the cost, how often production takes place, and the amount produced.

Large quantities of goods are distributed to distant areas. Some merchandise may even be distributed to consumers in other countries.

Products are distributed from the enterprise to wholesale and retail outlets all over the country by various means of transportation.

The retailer prepares the product sent to him by the enterprise for final distribution to the consumer.

Distribution may go even further with the consumer re-distributing the product to the consumers in her family.

Some form of distribution takes place within every type of enterprise.

Grocery stores are retailers who sell products directly to consumers.

CONTROLLING THE SYSTEM

No enterprise can remain in operation very long if it spends more money than it earns. This is a simple truth that applies to families, small businesses, and large corporations alike. The spending and earning of money must be **controlled** if the enterprise is to be a successful one. Controlling is accomplished in these four ways:

- Directing
- Checking
- Reporting
- Correcting

Controlling begins with the development of a plan that has specific goals.

SALES
COST OF GOODS
GROSS PROFIT
OPERATING EXPENSES
OPERATING INCOME
TAXES
NET INCOME

Enterprises direct the use of their finances to produce goods and provide services that will meet consumer needs.

DIRECTING THE ENTERPRISE

Bill and Mary Average realize the importance of controlling. With their two children they form one of the most common of all enterprises — the family. Bill and Mary work hard to keep their family financially successful. They both **direct** the use of their yearly income by creating a budget. The budget is a plan that lists the amounts of money to be spent on a number of items each month.

Bill and Mary have a monthly income of $900.00 from Bill's full-time and Mary's part-time jobs. This income must be used to meet the following monthly expenses.

Food. The Averages are careful shoppers in the grocery store so their food budget provides enough to feed the four of them. They allow **$210** a month (about **$52.50** per week) for food.

Housing. The Averages rent a home. Their monthly rent is **$220**.

Transportation. Bill drives the family car to work each day. Mary uses the city bus lines. Trips must also be made to the grocery store and for other errands. The Averages budget **$80** a month for transportation.

Clothing and Other Personal Items. Bill and Mary both need good clothing for their work. Their children outgrow their clothing every year. Everyone in the family needs toothpaste, soap, and other small items. The Averages spend **$100** each month in this area.

Medical Care. The Averages budget **$50** a month to pay for medicine, dental care, health insurance, and other such expenses.

Life Insurance. Bill pays $45 a month for life insurance. If something should happen to him, the insurance will help provide for Mary and the children.

Social Security. The budget allows $35 a month for Social Security. This is a government plan in which a certain amount of money is deducted from people's paychecks. It is put aside and saved for them until it is paid back in monthly amounts after they retire from work.

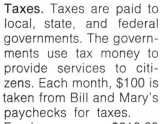

Taxes. Taxes are paid to local, state, and federal governments. The governments use tax money to provide services to citizens. Each month, $100 is taken from Bill and Mary's paychecks for taxes.

Food	$210.00
Housing	220.00
Transportation	80.00
Clothing and personal	$100.00
Medical care	50.00
Life insurance	45.00
Social Security	35.00
Taxes	$100.00
	$840.00

Parents, as managers of the family enterprise, control the use of their finances to meet daily needs.

In an enterprise staff members submit reports to their supervisors for examination and study.

The Averages have budgeted their income wisely. They earn $900.00 each month and use $840 to pay for their expenses.

Savings. Bill and Mary have budgeted the remaining $60 for their savings account each month. This money may later be used to buy a house or new car, pay for a vacation, or provide other things needed by the family. The money will earn **interest.** Interest is a percentage the savings company pays Bill and Mary for the use of their money as loans to other people during the year.

CHECKING, REPORTING, AND CORRECTING

From time to time, Bill and Mary will **check** their records of earning and spending to make sure they are following their budget as closely as possible. At the end of the year, the Averages sit down and write a complete **report** of their income and expenses. The report will show whether they experienced a **loss** by spending more money than they earned or made a **profit** by spending less than they earned.

First, the Averages look at their **total income** for the year — $10,800. They write this amount down. Then the Averages check their records to find the total amount of their yearly expenses.

Food	$2,520.00
Housing	2,640.00
Transportation	960.00
Clothing and other personal items	1,200.00
Medical care	600.00
Life insurance	540.00
Social Security	420.00
Taxes	1,200.00
Savings	720.00
Total yearly expenses	**$10,800.00**

Bill and Mary spent less money than what they earned. Actually, they made a profit, for they saved $720 because they planned their budget carefully.

Business enterprises must determine their profit and loss just as Mary and Bill did. Determining profit and loss in an enterprise is a much more complex process. A business must total its yearly income from the **sales** of its products or services. It must then determine the cost of producing the products or services it sold. It must total the expenses of operating the enterprise during the year. Taxes must be figured. The amount remaining after taxes is called the **net income.** Net income is the profit made by the enterprise.

Public enterprises, such as schools and government agencies, do not receive money from products or services. They must con-

Sales	$1,000,000
Cost of Goods Sold	–500,000
Research and Development. Royalties and Fees. Manufacturing. Plant Cost.	
Gross Profit on Sales	$ 500,000
Operating Expenses	–410,000
Administration. Selling. Promotion. Shipping and Delivery.	
Operating Income	$ 90,000
Taxes	–45,000
Net Income	$45,000

If reports indicate a need for corrective action, enterprise managers will direct what action needs to be taken.

At the end of the year, an enterprise must determine whether it has made a profit or loss.

trol their finances, however, so that they only spend the amount of money given to them by taxpayers and the government.

Elementary schools, for example, receive their income from local taxpayers and the state and federal governments. Schools must keep careful records of such costs as money spent for management and labor. Schools must also keep records that show their operating expenses. At the end of the year, the school's records are checked to make sure that the taxpayer's money was spent to provide good education. It must also be determined whether the school has spent more money than it received. If the school spent too much money, it must borrow more money and then use next year's taxes to pay it back.

CONTROLLING TO REMAIN IN OPERATION

You can see the importance of controlling the enterprise, whether it is a family, a private enterprise, or a public enterprise. By studying the amount of income it receives and the amount of money it spends to operate, an enterprise can decide whether it is spending more money than it receives through sales or a budget. An

The school administrator reviews the school budget with business personnel. Their objective is to make sure that the maximum amount of good education is received for each dollar spent in operating the enterprise.

enterprise or family must control its spending if it is to remain in operation.

REVIEWING YOUR VOCABULARY

selling	retailers
brand	wholesalers
sales person	directing
controlled	checking
promoting	reporting
promotion manager	correcting
advertising	budget
publicity	housing
influence	transportation
consumer market	life insurance
sterilize	taxes
inform	savings
media	loss
visual media	profit
audiovisual media	net income
direct selling	management
indirect selling	labor

INCREASING YOUR PERCEPTION

1. Explain the difference between publicity and advertising.
2. Develop a promotional plan using both advertising and publicity to sell consumers a child care product.
3. Define the words "selling" and "distributing."
4. Give examples of:
   a. Personal selling.
   b. Nonpersonal selling.
5. Identify and explain the different channels of distribution.
6. Discuss how a knowledge of selling techniques might help you as a consumer.
7. Define the word "profit" and the word "loss."
8. Explain why all enterprises, both public and private, must control their finances.
9. Work a sample profit and loss problem by selecting numbers to represent the costs of an enterprise that produces a toy such as a wagon.
10. Explain how you determine profit and loss in your personal life.

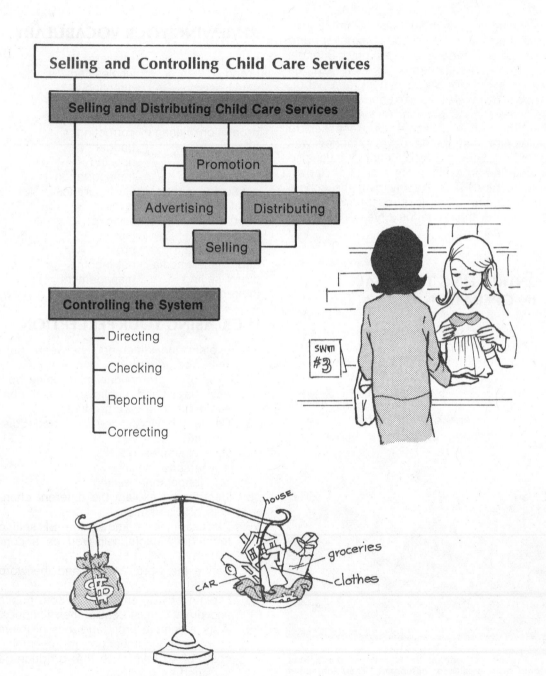

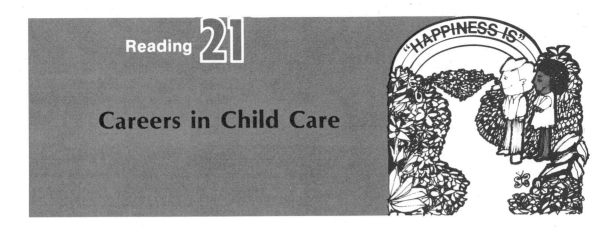

Careers in Child Care

"HAPPINESS IS"

Choosing a career is exciting — and one of the most important decisions you will make in your lifetime! When you choose the right career and you are satisfied and happy with the work you do, you will enjoy a sense of well-being and accomplishment. Making the wrong choice or making no real choice at all can lead to frustration and boredom. "If I had only . . .," is a sad and frequent beginning to many adults' discussions of their own working lives. By evaluating your abilities and interests now and gaining all the knowledge you can about available careers, you may never have to say, "If I had only . . . ."

Of all the careers available to people today, some of the most exciting can be found in child care. You may now have become interested in child care work and may be considering a career in the education, protection, or health care of children. There are thousands of different career opportunities in child care. Which occupation is best for you? **Organizing** child care careers and occupations may help you decide.

CLASSIFYING CAREERS TO FIND ONE FOR YOU

Most careers can be investigated by organizing them into three classifications: **working environment, working knowledge,** and **working skills.** By examining these classifications you may find the career that offers the opportuniites you seek.

WORKING ENVIRONMENT

How much you like an environment may determine in large measure how you feel about the work you do there. The **educational environment** is one of classrooms filled with children, books, learning, and discovering. You are already familiar with the educational environment because you have been a part of it for a long time. As an adult, would you enjoy working in an educational environment where you can help children learn and develop their abilities?

The **protection environment** is much different. It could be the tense atmosphere of a police headquarters or courtroom where a child's right to well-being and happiness is at stake. It might be a child and family service agency. The social worker's en-

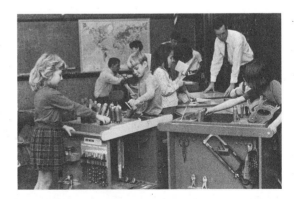

Would you enjoy working in the educational environment to help children form ideas about the kind of person they are, the kind of adult they would like to become, and the kind of career they might like to pursue?

vironment can be anywhere he or she is needed — a private home, a residential care center, an adoption agency, and sometimes in the sad atmosphere of a jail where a child is in trouble.

The **health environment** may be a hospital or clinic where human lives are being saved. In the environment of a hospital room, sick children can be restored to health. In a medical laboratory, chemicals, microscopes, and test tubes are the tools used daily to help children enjoy better health. Does the health care environment appeal to you?

If you choose to work in the protection environment, you might be responsible for placing children in suitable foster homes.

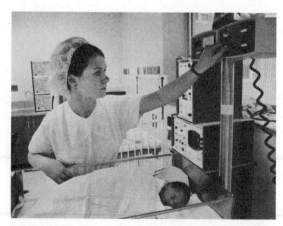

Working in the health environment may involve caring for newborn infants. Would you enjoy this environment?

WORKING KNOWLEDGE

In addition to environment, every career has its own working knowledge. For example, Ken is a kindergarten teacher. He must know how to present **educational** information in a way kindergarten children can understand. He must know how to evaluate each child's ability to learn. He must be able to recognize any special developmental problems that need attention. Would you enjoy learning about and working with this kind of educational knowledge?

Mary is a social worker at a child and family service agency. In order to help **protect** children, she must understand the problems that can harm relationships between family members. She must know how to help solve these problems. She has knowledge of how the human mind functions and can recognize signs of mental or social-emotional problems. Because Mary works closely with courts, she must also have knowledge of the laws of her state that protect families and children.

A working knowledge of children's needs is required in all child care careers. Do you understand children's needs?

Health care knowledge is concerned with the proper functioning of the human body and mind. Health care workers must know what treatments and what educational or rehabilitating actions can prevent or cure illness to keep the body in good health. Does the idea of having knowledge about the following items interest you?

disease	prescribing
medicine	pharmacy
surgery	vaccinations
therapy	prenatal care
examining	dentistry
diagnosing	laboratories

WORKING SKILLS

Finally, all careers have working skills. A skill is the ability to **use your knowledge to perform a task**. To provide children with **education** you would need the skills of planning programs for students, making lesson plans, creating or locating learning aids such as filmstrips, teaching, and evaluating each student's strengths and weaknesses. As a school principal, you would need the skills of managing the work of other people, controlling a budget, and creating good relations between your school and the community.

If you choose a career in **protection** you would often use skills of talking to people to help them with their problems. You would need to be able to skillfully direct troubled people to places where they can be helped. As a protection worker, you may also need the skill of keeping financial records, working with courts and law enforcement personnel, and even writing case studies. Do you feel that you could develop these skills?

If you would enter the **health care** field, you might find it necessary to learn how to take a medical history from a patient. You might also need the skill of analyzing a blood sample, giving a shot, or writing a prescription for medicine. Some health care workers must acquire the skill of keeping records of each patient's illnesses and treatment. Are you interested in learning these health care skills?

HUMAN WORK ACTIVITY

Every person uses **working skills when performing a human work activity**. The following human work activities are used in every enterprise:

- Researching information.
- Developing a product or a service.
- Preparing to provide.
- Providing a product or service.
- Selling.
- Managing.

While the same work activities are performed in almost all enterprises, the activities **produce different products and services**. Consider each of the human work activities carefully to decide **which one you would like to perform**.

RESEARCHING INFORMATION

Researching is one of the most important human work activities performed in enterprises. Research chemists **gather information** for new uses of plastics, foods, and fabrics. Enterprises depend upon marketing

If you were a day care center inspector, could you develop the working skills needed to check day care centers to ensure their safety for children?

researchers to use their research skills to identify the needs for child care products. Education researchers gather information to develop new methods of teaching effectively. Protection researchers conduct studies to design programs to reduce crimes or abuse of children. Psychologists gather information about children's social or emotional problems. Through their researching skills of **interviewing** and giving diagnostic **tests**, psychologists are able to guide troubled children and parents to better lives. Medical researchers conduct tests to **discover** new medicines or methods to prevent or cure diseases in children.

You might enjoy a career that performs the **researching** work activity if you like these skills:

- Identifying problems that need a solution.
- Gathering information.
- Conducting experiments.
- Classifying information.
- Using mathematics to analyze data.
- Reporting new ways of doing things.

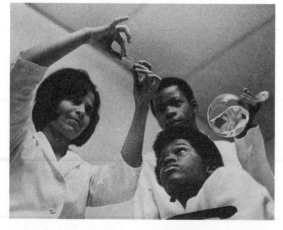

Would you enjoy experimenting to discover new ways of preparing or producing child care products?

DEVELOPING A PRODUCT OR SERVICE

The work activity of developing may be performed by designers who are skilled in using the information learned through research. They create new forms in children's clothing, toys, eating utensils, or educational programs. Drafting artists are skilled in producing **drawings** and **working models** of the designer's ideas. They also create **blueprints** from an architect's plan for a new school, home, or playground. Of course, products or services must be **tested** through surveying skills to make sure they will be successful.

Perhaps you are the kind of person who could perform the **developing** activities by using these skills:

- Using researched information.
- Thinking of creative ideas.
- Producing drawings of products or blueprints of buildings.
- Writing outlines of new service programs.
- Making product models.
- Testing with surveys.

PREPARING TO PROVIDE CHILD CARE

Preparing to produce products or provide services is an activity that demands the skills of workers who can organize people, equipment, and supplies to perform production processes. Production managers, for instance, must be skilled in gathering all the **resources** necessary for production and specifying the **work to be done.** They receive help from personnel directors who are skilled in **recruiting** and **hiring** workers. Personnel directors may also use their skills in handling **promotions** and **firings**, managing pay and vacation **policies**, organizing **insurance programs**, and setting up **training programs.** Purchasing agents are involved in preparing for production. They are skilled in **buying** the supplies, materials, and equipment needed by the enterprise. Receiving clerks must see that the items ordered by the purchasing agent arrive at the right time and are directed to the right department.

Can you see yourself performing the **preparing to produce** activity by using these skills:

- Gathering resources.
- Specifying.
- Recruiting and hiring workers.

- Preparing personnel training and other programs.
- Buying supplies, materials, and equipment.
- Receiving enterprise purchases.

PROVIDING A PRODUCT OR SERVICE

Providing is the activity that actually **makes a product or service ready for** the use of consumers. Teachers provide the

Perhaps you would enjoy recruiting and hiring personnel in preparation for production.

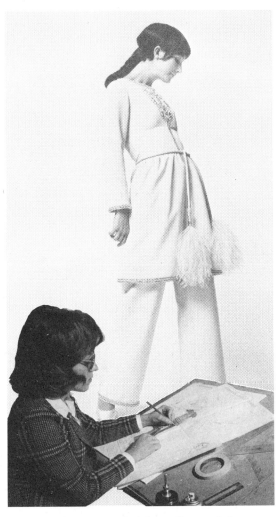

By using research information and her own ideas, the designer can "see" the finished product in her mind's eye and draw a rough sketch on paper. Does this designing activity appeal to you?

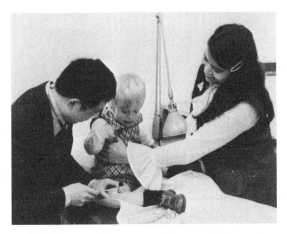

Skilled health care workers provide services to children by examining, diagnosing, prescribing, and treating. Would you be able to perform these activities?

education service by planning daily educational programs and by communicating those programs to students. Social workers and police provide protection by talking to children and adults, learning about their problems, and supplying them with the kind of services that will help solve their problems. Health care is provided by such people as physicians, therapists, and opticians through the skills of diagnosing, prescribing, and treating. Skilled workers who operate machinery in enterprises are also providing as they assemble products.

Now look at this checklist of skills needed to **provide** a product or service. Would performing these skills appeal to you?

- Creating a production plan.
- Communicating knowledge.
- Talking with people about their problems.
- Supplying the service that can help people solve their problems.
- Diagnosing an illness.
- Prescribing and treating an illness.
- Operating machinery.

SELLING CHILD CARE PRODUCTS OR SERVICES

The work activity of selling begins with the skill of the advertising worker who can **inform** consumers through pictures and words that products or services exist. Advertising workers are skilled at **influencing** the consumers to use the products or services. Sales people working directly for the enterprise or working in **retail** or **wholesale** trade areas actually sell the product or service to consumers. Sales people must understand the needs of the enterprise employing them and the needs of the consumers.

Selling might be your activity if you would enjoy using these skills:

- Creating pictures and words to inform and influence consumers.
- Placing advertisements in the media at the right time and place.
- Convincing consumers that a certain product or service will best meet their needs.

MANAGING THE CHILD CARE ENTERPRISE

The managing activity in the enterprise is done by people skilled in **planning, organizing,** and **controlling**. Some people are more skilled in managing other workers. The principal of a school or the director of a child and family service agency is mainly a manager of people. Other managers find their skills are best used in managing the

Selling is a communication skill — a way of informing and influencing consumers about a product or service. How good are your communication abilities?

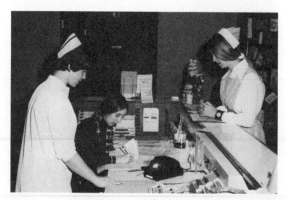

The head nurse must plan, organize, and control the duties and responsibilities of her staff. Could you manage people, data, and things well enough to do her job?

work of machines and the people who operate them. Managers of service enterprises deal with the planning, organizing, and controlling of services, but also must control the operation of school buses, medical equipment, and other machinery from time to time.

Are you a **manager**? You might be if you are skillful in these activities:

- Planning work to be done.
- Organizing the skills of other workers.
- Controlling the production of a job by seeing that each person or machine performs properly.

EMPLOYMENT OPPORTUNITIES

Because a career must be carefully selected, you will want to **match your**

Graduating from high school or college may be the first step in preparing for your employment opportunity.

talents and **abilities** to the career that fits you best. New careers are rapidly becoming available in child care occupations. More is being learned about children and their needs every day. This new knowledge creates the demand for more products and services. In the future, **you** may be one of those workers responsible for improving the lives of children through your career.

EDUCATION OPPORTUNITIES

Whether your skills are in the activities of researching, developing, preparing, providing, selling, or managing, **you can find an opportunity** to use them in a child care career in **education**. About two and a half million people are now teaching in schools in the United States. **Teachers** are very important education workers. They must usually complete college before beginning their careers. Some education employment opportunities exist in **school administration**. School **principals** and other **administrators** must also complete college and acquire additional experience and knowledge. Employment opportunities are present for other workers as well. **School nurses** usually have a college background, as well as having received hospital training. Of course, there are many more jobs in education that are not based on college training. A large number of opportunities exist for **bus drivers, maintenance workers,** and **teacher aides,** who acquire their skills through on-the-job training and orientation.

PROTECTION OPPORTUNITIES

An estimated 285 thousand police are only a small number of the people who have found employment opportunities in **protection**. **Police** employed in large cities first receive training in a police academy and then receive more training on the job itself. In smaller towns, police may be trained by a more experienced member of the force. About 160 thousand social workers and seven thousand urban planners also play a role in keeping the environment safe for

EMPLOYMENT OPPORTUNITIES

**GENERAL
WORK
ENVIRONMENTS**

**TRAINING
REQUIREMENTS**

	PROTECTION	EDUCATION	HEALTH	ANY ENVIRONMENT
UNIVERSITY EDUCATION	FBI agent parole officer social worker urban planner sociologist attorney day care operator criminologist	school counselor vocational counselor librarian teacher school administrator school principal educational researcher curriculum specialist	occupational therapist psychiatrist psychologist speech pathologist hospital administrator dentist dietician pharmacist physician nurse	accountant advertising worker economist market researcher personnel manager purchasing agent engineer manager writer chemist
SPECIAL TRAINING	detective fire fighter police officer legal secretary caseworker group worker day care teacher	library assistant paraprofessional	dental technologist dental hygienist medical technologist optician X-ray technician laboratory technician medical secretary practical nurse	bookkeeper clerk typist computer programmer secretary key punch operator draftsman electrician machinist bus driver cook salesperson
ON THE JOB TRAINING	day care aide homemaker's aide guard foster parent	library page teacher's aide	orderly attendant nurse's aide	custodian housekeeper telephone operator file clerk mail sorter cook assistant packager

You may select a career based upon a particular working environment or on the work activity performed.

children. Both social workers and urban planners are normally graduates of college. However, **case workers, drafting artists, secretaries, computer operators,** and some **court clerks** acquire their skills through special training or on-the-job experience. Many employment opportunities exist in protection.

HEALTH CARE OPPORTUNITIES

There are more than 200 different occupations in the **health care** environment. Over a million and a half people work at health jobs that improve the lives of children.

Physicians, dentists, pharmacists, and **speech therapists** must have college degrees to begin their careers. Some types of **nurses** have college training, while others are trained in hospitals. However, **nurse aides, cooks, laboratory assistants, X-ray technicians** — about a quarter of a million in all — usually do not have college degrees. Study the chart that shows the number of workers presently employed in health care and the number that will be needed in the future. Because of this need, your employment opportunity may be in health care.

Allied Health Manpower Requirements and Supply: 1967, 1975, and 1980

OCCUPATIONAL CATEGORY	ITEM	1967	1975	1980
TOTAL ALLIED HEALTH MANPOWER	Requirements	1,034,200	1,466,000	1,776,000
	Supply	806,500	1,144,000	1,372,000
	Deficit	227,700	322,000	404,000
AT LEAST A COLLEGE DEGREE				
Medical	Requirements	225,000	348,000	413,000
	Supply	175,000	270,000	320,000
	Deficit	50,000	78,000	93,000
Environmental	Requirements	105,000	135,000	155,000
	Supply	54,500	80,000	90,000
	Deficit	50,500	55,000	65,000
LESS THAN A COLLEGE DEGREE				
Medical	Requirements	336,500	488,000	580,000
	Supply	276,500	400,000	475,000
	Deficit	60,000	88,000	105,000
Dental	Requirements	165,700	203,000	246,000
	Supply	137,000	161,000	179,000
	Deficit	28,700	42,000	67,000
Environmental	Requirements	202,000	292,000	382,000
	Supply	163,500	233,000	308,000
	Deficit	38,500	59,000	74,000

Source: Public Health Service estimates.

Note: Figures in this table do not include licensed practical nurses, nurse aides, orderlies, or attendants.

YOUR DECISION

You have had the opportunity to explore careers in child care. By attempting to see yourself working in a particular **environment** and by using **knowledge** and **skills** to perform human work activities, you are now **better prepared** to make **your own career decision.**

REVIEWING YOUR VOCABULARY

Your employment may provide on-the-job training at the same time you are earning money.

career
occupations
classifications
working environment
working knowledge
working skills
atmosphere
rehabilitating
human work activity
researching
developing
preparing
providing
selling
managing
diagnostic tests
survey skills
specifying
teachers
school principals
administrators

bus drivers
maintenance workers
teacher aides
police
social workers
urban planners
case workers
drafting artists
secretaries
computer operators
court clerks
physicians
dentists
pharmacists
speech therapists
nurses
nurse aides
cooks
laboratory assistant
x-ray technicians
employment
    opportunities

INCREASING YOUR PERCEPTION

1. Identify careers in the health environment, the education environment, and the protection environment.

2. List as many occupations as you can that perform each of the human work activities or a combination of the work activities.
3. Identify occupations where personnel work with people, things, data, or a combination of these three.
4. Give examples of working knowledge and working skills in each working environment.
5. Select six workers from one working environment and identify the training or education needs of each worker.
6. Identify career opportunities in health, education, and protection enterprises in your community.

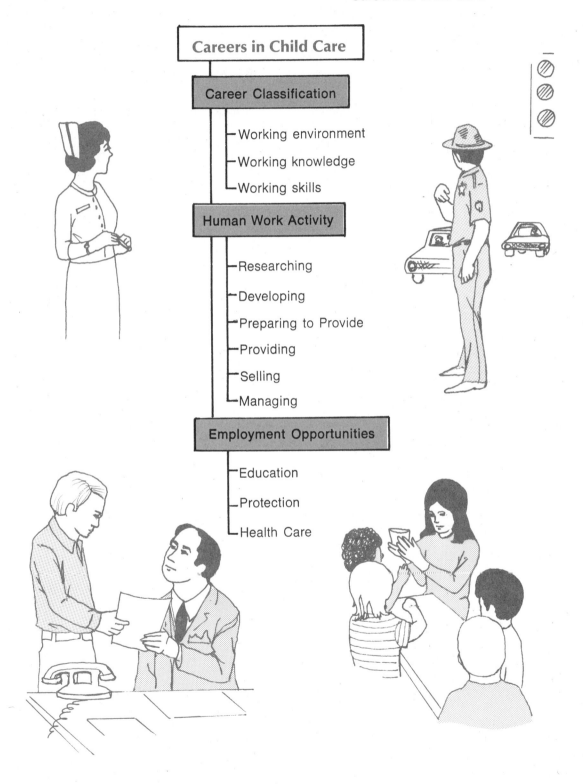

Careers in Child Care

Career Classification
- Working environment
- Working knowledge
- Working skills

Human Work Activity
- Researching
- Developing
- Preparing to Provide
- Providing
- Selling
- Managing

Employment Opportunities
- Education
- Protection
- Health Care

Entering the World of Work

What will you be doing for the rest of your life? Have you really thought about it? You can reasonably expect to live at least 50 more years. That is a long time! What will you do with the years that belong to you? How you answer this question will determine, to a great degree, how happy and satisfying your life will be.

Because your life belongs to you, **you** alone have the responsibility of choosing the kind of life that suits you best. **You** must determine the way you want to live and the career you want to follow during the years that lie ahead of you.

Selecting a career may seem a little frightening — there are so many different careers. Many individuals find themselves wondering, "Where do I fit in?" You can turn that question around and ask yourself, "What career fits **me**?" To answer that question, you must first know who **you** are.

SELECTING A LIFESTYLE

If you have watched individual athletes very closely or studied the works of different artists or writers, you have probably noticed that each had a particular way of performing his or her sport or craft. That particular way is called **style**. Hank Aaron has his own style of playing baseball. Ernest Hemingway had his own style of writing. Billie Jean King has her style of playing tennis. You have your own style of living. It is called your **lifestyle**.

You must know your goals and abilities before you can select a career that is just right for you.

FAMILY

Your lifestyle reflects how you **value** certain things. What you value tells a lot about you as a person. How much do you value family, for example? Do you enjoy spending time with your family? Are family picnics or other social events important to you? Some people choose to make family the central point of their lifestyle while other people choose different things. What do you choose?

FRIENDS

Just about everyone wants and needs **friends**. However, friends are more important to some people than they are to others. When you finish school for the day, do you spend your free time with friends? Or, perhaps you are the kind of person who sometimes prefers to read a book or work on a project by yourself? What kind of friends do you enjoy? The type of lifestyle you select

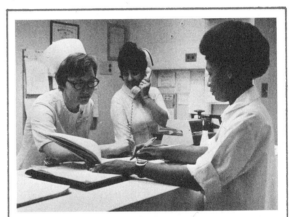

How important you consider your family determines what part it plays in your newly emerging lifestyle.

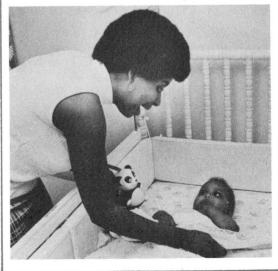

You determine how much your friends will influence your lifestyle.

When you choose a lifestyle that includes both a family and a career, you must plan carefully to meet both responsibilities.

will be one of the major factors in your choice of friends. Friends may mean a lot to you, but will you make them the most important part of your lifestyle?

PERSONAL WELL-BEING

Personal well-being plays a big part in each individual's lifestyle. Think carefully. What is it that makes you feel really good about yourself and the world in which you live? Is it a certain religious belief? Is it trying something you have never done before, or is it completing a very difficult task? Does a sense of security give you personal well-being or does helping other people give you the satisfied feeling? How you feel about yourself will affect all other areas of your life. If you really know and like yourself, you will have a positive attitude toward life and will be more successful in achieving your lifestyle goals.

LEISURE ACTIVITIES

How do you feel about leisure activities? What you do in your leisure time can greatly affect your style of life. You may enjoy a sport such as tennis or a craft such as ceramics so much that it will always be more important to you than any other activity. If so, you probably would not want a career that would shorten your leisure time to enjoy this activity. On the other hand, you could be the type of person who cares very little about **leisure** activities because your career is much more exciting and important, or because you want to spend your free time in volunteer service to the community.

Sometimes you may feel like being by yourself — enjoying the world around you and finding peace and contentment. What part will personal well-being have in your lifestyle?

Leisure-time activities include such things as music, sports, art, or just "doing your thing." How much value you place on them will affect your lifestyle.

CAREER

Because you will probably work at least 40 hours a week, your **career** will play a big role in your lifestyle. Do you think you would like to spend 40 hours a week or more in the education, protection, or health care environment? You may be the kind of person who really enjoys the atmosphere of the classroom or administrative office. If you are an active person who likes variety and a little excitement, police work or social work could be your environment. Can you imagine yourself as a laboratory technician in a health care world of test tubes and chemicals? Selecting your career is an important decision because you should choose one that allows you to meet other life style goals that you value. For example, a career should not

Unless you also enjoy your career environment, you may feel "stuck" in a position that is non-productive and boring.

force you to totally give up spending time with your family or leisure activity if that is what you value.

WORK ACTIVITY

What kind of work activity would really fit the style of life you want to develop? Would gathering informaiton as a **research** chemist or psychologist allow you to develop your sense of well being? **Developing** products and services as a designer is an exciting activity. Would you, however, be able to make the type of friends you enjoy in such a career? **Preparing to produce** might place you in the role of production manager. Would such an activity help you or make it difficult for you to achieve the type of family life you want? Teachers, doctors, and skilled machine operators **provide products** and **services**. If you want a great deal of leisure time, would you have it as a doctor or teacher? a machine operator? **Selling** may place you behind the counter in a large department store or require you to travel

The selection of a career that matches your lifestyle is the most important decision you will make.

across the country. Will this kind of work activity help you achieve the lifestyle you wish? **Managers** must plan, organize, and control the work that other people perform. It can be a career that requires most of your time and effort. Would your lifestyle fit this career? You can see from these examples how selecting the human work activity you want to perform must be done carefully to achieve both the career satisfaction and the lifestyle you desire.

SELECTING A CAREER

You probably have not definitely decided what kind of lifestyle you want. Your choices will develop over a period of time. This is also true of your career. It may be a number of years before you know exactly what career will best fit your interests, abilities, and talents. However, you should begin to **plan, organize,** and **control** your activities during your school years so that you can achieve your career goals in the future.

PLANNING CAREER GOALS

You can plan for the education and experience needed for your future career by taking the necessary courses in school,

taking a part-time job in career areas that interest you, and by talking with someone who works in your career field.

During her last year in junior high school, for example, Linda became very interested in law. She felt that she might like to become a lawyer. Linda took several courses in government and social studies in high school. She also visited a lawyer to talk about this possible career. The lawyer explained to Linda the kind of education required for the career and the kind of work a lawyer does each day. During the summers, Linda worked part time as a filing clerk in the lawyer's office. She discovered for herself what the environment was like, as well as earning money to save toward her future education. Because she had tested the environment, Linda knew this was the career she wanted.

ORGANIZING CAREER GOALS

You can **organize** by developing a good plan of action. You must know what direction to take in preparing for a particular career and how to reach your career goal.

Planning what courses to study in school is one of the first steps in making a career choice.

Talk over your career plans with someone who works in the occupation you have chosen.

Few people have become successful by just drifting along with no future plans. You must know where you are going and how you will get there. Linda's plan was to become a lawyer who would help people who had very little money. To put her plan into action, she took courses in high school that would prepare her for the college training she would need as a lawyer. She also saved money from the summer job and applied for a scholarship to attend a university with an exceptionally good law school division.

```
                PERSONAL AND CONFIDENTIAL RÉSUMÉ

Walter Smith
1403 Pleasant Drive
Normal, Illinois  61761
452-7593

TYPE OF POSITION SOUGHT:

    Educational Research Coordinator

EXPERIENCE:

    9/70 to 6/73

    Teacher - Grades 4 and 5, Cooper Elementary School, 409 West Linden,
    Lincoln, Illinois.

    6/69 to 8/70

    Graduate Assistant, University of Illinois, Urbana, Illinois, Super-
    vised student teachers.

    9/65 to 6/69

    Assistant Researcher Librarian, Milner Library, Illinois State University,
    Normal, Illinois - gathered materials for use by instructors and pro-
    fessors, sorted, cataloged, and filed research materials.

    1/69 to 4/69

    Conducted survey on use of library materials by students and faculty.

EDUCATION:

    Illinois State University, Normal, Illinois              1966-69
    Major:  Education, Bachelor of Science in Education

    University of Illinois, Urbana, Illinois                 1969-70
    Major:  Education Research, Master of Science in Education

OUTSIDE ACTIVITIES:

    Member of Community Beautification Committee, Program Director for local
    ski club, golf, tennis, member of Community Library Board.

PERSONAL DATA:

    Birthdate:  October 20, 1945        Weight:  170 lbs.
    Place of birth:  Bloomington, Illinois    Marital Status:  Married
    Height:  6' 1"                      Citizenship:  U.S. Citizen

REFERENCES:

    References and record of courses and grades will be furnished upon re-
    quest.
```

Past experiences may be organized and recorded in a resume which gives an employer information about your education and work experience.

CONTROLLING CAREER GOALS

Finally, you can **control** your progress toward your goal by following your plan. If the plan proves to be unrealistic — that is, if your goals seem out of reach — change your goal and make new plans. Linda, for example, discovered during college that she did not have the abilities needed to be a lawyer. She still wanted to help people however, so she changed her studies to become a social worker.

Selecting a career that demands additional training or education may mean that you will have to compromise. This means it might be necessary to postpone achievement of other goals such as marriage or material goods while you take the additional training to prepare for your selected career. If you choose the career of doctor, for example, you may have to give up plans for a new car or a family until you have completed the seven or more years of education and training required to be licensed as a physician. Would you be willing to compromise or postpone other personal goals to achieve your career goal?

Control the direction of your career by following your plan to gain the experience and knowledge that will prepare you for your career choice.

CAREER OPPORTUNITY

Once you decide upon a certain career, how do you actually enter that field? You may do as Karen did. She found a **short-term** career opportunity that helped her reach her final goal. Karen wanted to become a writer of children's books. However, she felt that she needed to learn writing skills and self-discipline first. Therefore, Karen found a job as a reporter for a small newspaper. She did not plan to remain at the newspaper for a long time. While there she learned the self-discipline required by knowing she must meet schedules in submitting her newspaper articles. The job was a short-term opportunity that enabled her to learn the skills and improve personal development necessary for the achievement of her career goal.

Many people have begun their careers by accepting short-term opportunities. Others have taken long-term opportunities. After graduating from college with a degree in social work, Bob began his career with a child and family service agency. Bob planned to be in social work all of his life. He saw his position with the agency as the beginning of a long commitment to helping others. Both Bob and Karen achieved their career goals — they simply reached them through different avenues.

If you choose your career wisely, it will become an important part of your life and will bring you self-respect and a feeling of accomplishment. To do this, you must first discover the kind of lifestyle you wish. You must then select a career in the world of work that will match your abilities, talents,

A candy striper (volunteer health care worker) receives on-the-job training in a short-term job that will help her prepare for a long-term medical career.

The future is yours — as well as the responsibility of making that future life happy and satisfying.

and lifestyle. You must plan your goals, organize your plan of action, and control your progress to achieve those goals. Always remember — your life belongs to you. Will it be an exciting, rewarding one? That is your choice. Think about it. What will you be doing for the **rest of your life?**

REVIEWING YOUR VOCABULARY

lifestyle

family

friends

personal well-being

leisure activities

career environment

human work activity

plan

organize

control

scholarship

unrealistic

compromise

postpone

material goods

personal goals

short-term

career opportunity

long term

INCREASING YOUR PERCEPTION

1. Define the meaning of the word "lifestyle."
2. Describe your lifestyle now and what you hope it will be in 10 years.
3. Identify the factors to consider in choosing your lifestyle.
4. Explain how a choice of careers can affect your lifestyle.
5. Explain how compromise may be involved in a career choice.
6. Explain how you can begin now to plan, organize, and control your future.
7. Identify the difference between short-and long-term career opportunities.
8. Develop your career exploration plans for the next three years.

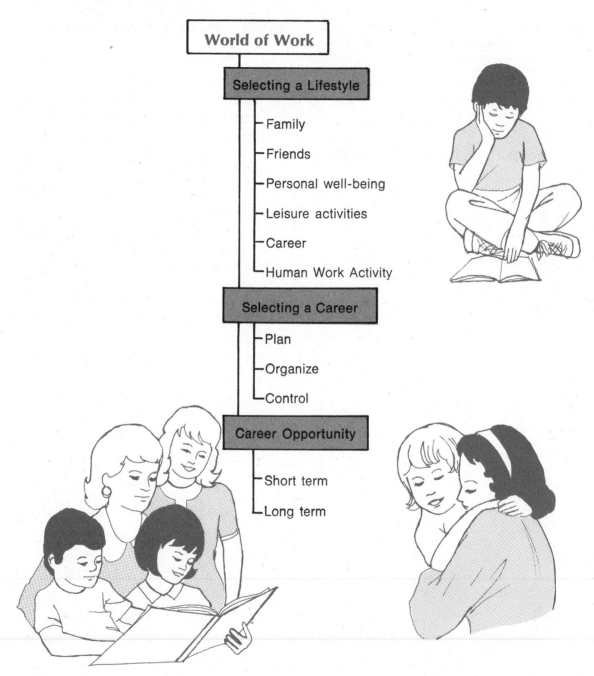

World of Work

Selecting a Lifestyle
- Family
- Friends
- Personal well-being
- Leisure activities
- Career
- Human Work Activity

Selecting a Career
- Plan
- Organize
- Control

Career Opportunity
- Short term
- Long term

Index

Mental illness —
  diagnosing, 142
  needs of, 58
  and safety, 113
Mentally retarded, 119
Messages —
  receiving, 40
  silent, 36
Methods, educational, 77-88
Ministers, 109, 110, 125
Miranda warning, 108, 113
Misunderstanding, 40
Model, working, 178
Money, 175
  in enterprise, 52
  for kindergarten, 42
  to provide children's
    needs, 20
Mortality rate, 128
Mother, prenatal care, 129
Mouth-to-mouth
  resuscitation, 149
Mumps, 144
Muscular dystrophy, 155
Myopia, 139

Needs —
  caring for a child's daily,
    23-33
  and community living,
    16-22
  consumer, 165
  determining protection,
    109
  diagnosing, 63
  educational, 56-65
  exploring human, 1-7
  exploring personal, 8-15
  health, 128-130, 139
  meeting health care,
    147-158
  physical, 1-2
  for protection, 99-107
  resources used to meet
    children's, 20
  social-emotional, 2-3
Neglected children, 117
Net income, 192
Nurse, 23, 43, 70, 75, 104, 153,
    156, 157, 180
Nurses' aides, 157, 203

Objective, see Goals
Obsession, 145
Obstetrician, 23

Occupations, 1
  early, 16
Ophthalmologist, 133, 139, 140
Orderly, 154, 157
Organizing, 200
  career plan, 211
  kindergarten, 43-44
Ownership —
  education as, 93
  of enterprise, 161
  hospital, 152
  sole, 49

Pacemaker, 179
Paraprofessional, 43
Parents —
  adoptive, 113, 121
  and children's needs,
    23-33
  diagnose and prescribe,
    139, 142
  educational role, 58
  provide children's needs,
    18-19
  safety education, 150
Partnership, 49, 162
Pediatrician, 28, 153
People —
  for enterprise, 163
  to provide children's
    needs, 20
Performing, in learning, 89, 93
Personal goals, 13-14
Personal needs, 8-15
Personal well-being, 208
Personnel, selecting,
    171-183
Personnel work, 198
Pharmacist, 143, 203
Phenylketonuria, 24
Phonics, 84
Physical education, 69, 86
Physical examination, 129
Physical needs, 1-2, 57
Physical safety, 110
Physical therapist, 70, 125, 155,
    156
Physician see Doctors
Plan, of production, 177
Planning, 200
  career, 211
  for kindergarten, 42
  of lesson, 80
  to meet child's needs,
    23-25

need for, 52
  protection, 108, 115
  value of, 179
Plaque, 166
Play, as education, 28-31, 67
Pneumonia, 130
Poison, 141
Police, 108, 111, 122, 195
  careers, 201
  and protection needs, 101
Policy, of enterprise, 162
Policies —
  setting, 50
Polio, 155
Practice, in learning, 89, 92
Praise, need of, 13
Prenatal care, 129
Prescribing, 66-76, 147
  health care, 139-146
Prescription, 66
Primary grades, 69, 84
Principal, 74
Private ownership, 152, 162
  type, 161
Process, education as, 96
Producing, 209
Products —
  child care, 159
  distributing, 181
  making, 179, 199
  preparing to make, 209
  testing, 167
Production, 179
  preparing for, 198
Profit, 50, 192
Program —
  educational, 69
  for kindergarten, 43
  planned educational, 81-83
Promotion, manager, 184
Proprietorship, sole, 49, 162
Protection, 160
  careers in, 201
  children's needs, 99-107,
    108-115
  community needs of, 17
  environment of, 195
  human need of, 2
  providing, 18-19, 116-127
  providing child's daily,
    25-27
  skills used, 197
Psychiatrist, 105, 144
Psychologist, 70, 114, 119, 125,
    143, 144, 198